Selected Speeches and Writings of

NELSON MANDELA

The End of Apartheid in South Africa

Red and Black Publishers, St Petersburg, Florida

Library of Congress Cataloging-in-Publication Data

Mandela, Nelson, 1918-
    [Selections. 2010]
    Selected speeches and writings of Nelson Mandela : the end of apartheid in
South Africa.
        p. cm.
    ISBN 978-1-934941-78-2
1. South Africa--Politics and government--1948-1994--Sources. 2. South Africa--
Politics and government--1994---Sources. 3. Apartheid--South Africa--History--
Sources. 4. Anti-apartheid movements--South Africa--History--20th century--Sources.
5. African National Congress--History--20th century--Sources. 6. South Africa--Race
relations--Sources. 7. Blacks--South Africa--Politics and government--Sources. I.
Title.
    DT1974.M344 2010
    352.23'80968--dc22

                                                                2010000667

Red and Black Publishers, PO Box 7542, St Petersburg, Florida, 33734
Contact us at: info@RedandBlackPublishers.com
        Printed and manufactured in the United States of America

Contents

Editor's Preface

Nelson Rolihlala Mandela was born in July 1918, in the Transkei province of South Africa. His father, Henry Mandela, was a chieftain of the Tembu tribe, and the young Nelson was being groomed for a high position in the tribe, but instead left to study law.

In 1948, the New Nationalist Party, made up mostly of Afrikaners, or descendents of Dutch settlers, won the elections, and imposed a rigid social system of racism and white supremacy onto the country that was known as *apartheid* ("separateness"). The Nationalists would hold power for almost the next half century.

Under the Prohibition of Mixed Marriages Act and the Immorality Amendment, mixed marriages and interracial sex were outlawed; under the Abolition of Passes Act, Africans were required to carry an identifying passbook at all times, and could not move from one area to another without permission; under the Population Registration Act, the entire population was registered by racial group (into "White", "Bantu", "Indian" or "Coloured"); under the Group Areas Act, land areas were assigned by race, and people who lived in the "wrong" areas were forcibly removed and "resettled"; under the Reservation of

Separate Amenities Act, public amenities such as beaches, swimming pools and restaurants were segregated; under the Separate Representation of Voters Act, the right to vote was restricted solely to Whites; and under the Bantu Education Act, a separate education system was set up for Blacks (but controlled entirely by Whites) to give "appropriate" teaching to the different racial groups.

To enable control of the majority of the population by the white minority, South Africa was turned into a police state. The Suppression of Communism Act allowed the government to outlaw any "subversive" organization, while both individuals and organizations were subject to "banning orders" which prohibited them from writing, speaking publicly, or attending public meetings. The Terrorism Act established the Bureau of State Security (BOSS), which had authority to jail "terrorists" (anyone who criticized apartheid) indefinitely without trial.

The ultimate stage of the apartheid policy was the formation of "Bantu Homelands", which were small areas set aside as "independent states" for the African population. In theory, each of the "homelands" was to be a place where each African tribe could have independence and self-rule, and all Africans were involuntarily stripped of South African citizenship and assigned to a "homeland". In reality, however, the homelands were simply huge prison camps, which served to remove the Africans from White presence until they were needed as pools of cheap labor. None of the world's nations ever recognized the legality of the homeland "governments".

Appalled by the injustice of the apartheid system, Mandela and his partner, Oliver Tambo, set up the first Black law firm in Johannesburg, specializing in defending poverty-stricken clients who were accused of violating the apartheid laws. Both Mandela and Tambo were members of the African National Congress, an organization dedicated to democracy and an end to institutionalized racism. By 1952, the ANC was South Africa's leading anti-apartheid organization, and Mandela was directing its Youth League. One of the most vehement opponents of apartheid was the outlawed South African Communist Party, which formed an alliance with the ANC that lasted through the entire era. Mandela became friends with many members of the Communist Party's underground leadership.

Mandela became impressed by the work of Mohandas Gandhi, an immigrant from India who was resisting apartheid in the Indian and Coloured communities by organizing mass actions of nonviolent non-cooperation. In 1952, Mandela helped organize the Campaign for the Defiance of Unjust Laws, a civil disobedience campaign to resist the pass laws. He was arrested and convicted, then given a suspended sentence. Mandela was also told that his law practice was illegal, since it was not located in the proper racial neighborhood, and he was ordered to leave Johannesburg. Instead, he defied the order and remained in the city illegally. In 1955, Mandela helped to write the Freedom Charter, which summarized the ANC's program of a non-racial democracy and became the central document of the anti-apartheid movement.

In March 1956, Mandela was served with a banning order, prohibiting him from writing, speaking or traveling. In December, he and 100 other anti-apartheid activists were arrested and charged with treason—the trial was designed to simply harass the activists, and Mandela was finally acquitted of the charges in 1961.

In 1960, another anti-apartheid group, the Pan-Africanist Congress (PAC), called a peaceful mass protest in Sharpeville against the pass laws. Police fired on the unarmed demonstrators, killing 70 people. Shortly later, the apartheid government, which had been an independent nation within the British commonwealth (like Canada or Australia), left the commonwealth and pronounced a Republic of South Africa. The ANC replied by organizing a stay-at-home "general strike", which was immediately the focus of intense police and military repression. Shortly after, the ANC was banned by the South African government.

Forced into hiding, the ANC leadership decided that peaceful nonviolent protest was useless against a regime that was willing to machine-gun unarmed women and children, and the ANC decided to organize an underground military wing to carry out armed guerrilla actions against the regime. Mandela was chosen to carry out the work. The new organization was called Umkhonto we Sizwe ("Spear of the Nation"). Mandela, its commander in chief, knew nothing whatever about military matters, and, when the West refused to help him, turned instead to the South African Communist Party and its contacts in the Soviet Bloc. In 1962, Mandela left the country illegally and traveled to through Africa to Ethiopia, making arrangements for Soviet-supplied weapons and training for his guerrilla fighters.

Upon his return to South Africa, Mandela was arrested and charged with illegally leaving the country and of organizing the stay-at-home strike. He was sentenced to five years of hard labor. While in prison, in 1963, Mandela and dozens of other anti-apartheid activists were charged with treason in the "Rivonia Trial", named after the Johannesburg suburb where most of them were arrested. Mandela's statement to the court, a passionate condemnation of apartheid, became famous worldwide. Although the apartheid government had sought the death penalty, international pressure forced them to impose a life sentence instead. Mandela and the others were sent to the maximum security prison on Robben Island. He stayed there for the next 27 years.

During the time Mandela was in prison, the anti-apartheid movement grew in stature and influence, and soon reached an international stage. South Africa became an outlaw pariah state, shunned by most of the international community. In 1962, the United Nations passed Resolution 1761, declaring apartheid to be criminal. In 1963, the UN formed a Special Committee Against Apartheid. The International Olympics Committee voted to exclude South Africa from the Games. In 1974, the General Assembly passed a resolution to expel South Africa from the UN, but the action was vetoed by France, England and the United States. In 1977, after police massacred hundreds of unarmed student protesters in Soweto, the UN placed an arms embargo on South Africa.

Under a policy called "constructive engagement", the Reagan and Thatcher Administrations continued to prop up the Pretoria regime. American and British corporations were supported in their dealings with South Africa, under the theory that they could then presumably help to "influence" South African policy away from apartheid. The South African government was particularly dependent upon American-made computer technology, without which the bureaucratic task of administrating the maze of apartheid laws and classifications would have been impossible. Both Thatcher and Reagan classified the ANC as "communist" and a "terrorist organization", and ANC members were banned from entering the US without special permission.

In the United States, opponents of the apartheid regime organized a nation-wide campaign for "divestment", calling on companies and governments to cut off all economic ties to South Africa. Although American corporations (and the Reagan Administration) resisted the divestment movement, thousands of local and state governments in the US passed laws forbidding economic cooperation with South Africa. There were also increasing international pressures on South Africa to release Mandela and other imprisoned activists.

By the 1980's, the growing effectiveness of the ANC, and the increasingly hostile international isolation of South Africa, led to a siege mentality within the Pretoria government. President PW Botha surrounded himself with generals and police officials and became obsessed with security. His actions became increasingly more militaristic.

The African nations that bordered South Africa became known as "the front-line states". Not only were they providing refuge for exiled anti-apartheid activists and ANC guerrillas, but, as examples of Black-led states, they were ideologically repugnant to the Afrikaner white supremacists. South African military incursions into the frontline states steadily escalated, from small cross-border raids on ANC bases, to military and political support for Pretoria-friendly guerrilla groups like UNITA in Angola and FRELIMO in Mozambique, to military operations against the ANC ally SWAPO (South West Africa People's Organization, which was fighting to end South Africa's illegal occupation of Namibia), to, finally, a full-scale invasion of Angola. South Africa even secretly produced a small number of nuclear weapons, to be used as a last resort against apartheid's enemies.

By the 1970's, however, the inevitable end of apartheid was already in sight. The enormous costs of administrating and defending the apartheid system were a huge drain on the economy—a situation that was exacerbated by increasing international sanctions (in 1985, Botha defiantly announced that he would never allow the white minority in South Africa to commit "suicide" through black rule, and, faced with Botha's intransigence, even the US and Britain were finally forced to give in to pressure to place economic sanctions on South Africa).

By 1983, the South African economy was a shambles, the political situation was more unstable than ever, and the need to make reforms was unstoppable. Botha introduced a new Constitution containing a Tricameral Parliament, in which Indians and Coloureds would now have their own legislative bodies. These would have authority to administrate (and pay for) its own "internal affairs" such as education or health care. National matters would still be decided by the white-dominated Cabinet. Africans were to have no representation at all in the government; they were considered to be "citizens" of their "Bantustan homelands"—their passbooks would be repealed, and they would now be issued "passports" from their "homeland". Henceforth, Africans would only be treated as "foreign guest workers".

Botha began making covert overtures to Mandela, hoping to use him to gain credibility for the Bantustans. In 1984, Botha sent word that he was willing release Mandela from prison, on the condition that he make a public announcement accepting the legitimacy of the Transkei "homeland" and agree to live there. Mandela refused. A year later, while Mandela was recuperating from surgery in prison, Botha secretly sent another offer, saying he would release Mandela if he would renounce armed struggle. Mandela again refused, but he was transferred from Robben Island prison to the lower-security Victor Verser prison farm.

In 1989, Botha suffered a stroke, and FW de Klerk replaced him as President of South Africa. It was a turning point, as de Klerk realized that the entire system of apartheid was breaking down and could not be saved. In February 1990, de Klerk issued an order un-banning the ANC, the South African Communist Party, the Pan-Africanist Congress, and other anti-apartheid organizations. Nine days later, Mandela was released from prison, after serving 27 years. He was promptly elected President of the ANC.

The collapse of apartheid began. De Klerk agreed to the release of all political prisoners, began dismantling all the legal machinery of apartheid, and ordered the formation of a Convention for a Democratic South Africa (CODESA) to draw up a non-racial constitution. De Klerk, however, bowing to pressure from the Afrikaner nationalists, insisted that a three-fourths vote be required for any constitutional changes. Since this could not be done without the cooperation of the Nationalist Party, this would in effect give the White minority virtual veto power. Negotiations came to an impasse.

This was followed by a wave of violence. Peaceful protestors in the Ciskei "Bantu Homeland", who were demanding the reintegration of Ciskei back into South Africa, were fired upon by "homeland" police. At the same time, violent confrontations were taking place between ANC supporters and members of the Zulu-based Inkatha Freedom Party, which wanted to set up an independent Zulu nation in the KwaZulu "homeland". There was also violence from whites who feared black rule; South African Communist Party leader Chris Hani was assassinated in April 1993 by a white nationalist.

When negotiations restarted, de Klerk finally gave in and agreed to elections for a new democratic government on the basis of "one person, one vote".

In April 27, 1994 ("Freedom Day"), South Africa's first free election was won by the African National Congress, with 62% of the vote. Nelson Mandela was sworn in as President.

For their joint work in ending apartheid, both Mandela and FW de Klerk shared the 1993 Nobel Peace Prize. Mandela is now viewed worldwide as a symbol of human freedom, and has received numerous other awards and honors, including the Prince of Asturias Prize of International Co-Operation, the Felix Houphouet-Boigny Peace Prize, the Sakharov Prize for Freedom of Thought by the European Parliament, the Order of Merit from Queen Elizabeth, the Medal of Freedom from President George W Bush, the OAU's Africa Peace Award, the Gandhi Peace Prize from India, the Ataturk Prize from Turkey (which he refused to accept because of Turkey's human rights violations), and the very last Lenin Peace Prize to be awarded by the Soviet Union before its collapse.

"No Easy Walk to Freedom"

September 21, 1953

Since 1912 and year after year thereafter, in their homes and local areas, in provincial and national gatherings, on trains and buses, in the factories and on the farms, in cities, villages, shanty towns, schools and prisons, the African people have discussed the shameful misdeeds of those who rule the country. Year after year, they have raised their voices in condemnation of the grinding poverty of the people, the low wages, the acute shortage of land, the inhuman exploitation and the whole policy of white domination. But instead of more freedom, repression began to grow in volume and intensity and it seemed that all their sacrifices would end up in smoke and dust. Today the entire country knows that their labours were not in vain, for a new spirit and new ideas have gripped our people. Today the people speak the language of action: there is a mighty awakening among the men and women of our country and the year 1952 stands out as the year of this upsurge of national consciousness.

In June, 1952, the African National Congress and the South African Indian Congress, bearing in mind their responsibility as the representatives of the downtrodden and oppressed people of South Africa, took the plunge and launched the Campaign for the Defiance of the Unjust Laws. Starting off in Port Elizabeth in the early hours of June 26 and with only thirty-three defiers in action and then in Johannesburg in the afternoon of the same day with one hundred and six defiers, it spread throughout the country like wild fire. Factory and office workers, doctors, lawyers, teachers, students and the clergy; Africans, Coloureds, Indians and Europeans, old and young, all rallied to the national call and defied the pass laws and the curfew and the railway apartheid regulations. At the end of the year, more than 8,000 people of all races had defied. The Campaign called for immediate and heavy sacrifices. Workers lost their jobs, chiefs and teachers were expelled from the service, doctors, lawyers and businessmen gave up their practices and businesses and elected to go to jail. Defiance was a step of great political significance. It released strong social forces which affected thousands of our countrymen. It was an effective way of getting the masses to function politically; a powerful method of voicing our indignation against the reactionary policies of the Government. It was one of the best ways of exerting pressure on the Government and extremely dangerous to the stability and security of the State. It inspired and aroused our people from a conquered and servile community of yes-men to a militant and uncompromising band of comrades-in-arms. The entire country was transformed into battle zones where the forces of liberation were locked up in immortal conflict against those of reaction and evil. Our flag flew in every battlefield and thousands of our countrymen rallied around it. We held the initiative and the forces of freedom were advancing on all fronts. It was against this background and at the height of this Campaign that we held our last annual provincial Conference in Pretoria from the 10th to the 12th of October last year. In a way, that Conference was a welcome reception for those who had returned from the battlefields and a farewell to those who were still going to action. The spirit of defiance and action dominated the entire conference.

Today we meet under totally different conditions. By the end of July last year, the Campaign had reached a stage where it had to be suppressed by the Government or it would impose its own policies on the country.

The government launched its reactionary offensive and struck at us. Between July last year and August this year forty-seven leading members from both Congresses in Johannesburg, Port Elizabeth and Kimberley were arrested, tried and convicted for launching the Defiance Campaign and given suspended sentences ranging from three months to two years, on condition that they did not again participate in the defiance of the unjust laws. In November last year, a proclamation was passed which prohibited meetings of more than ten Africans and made it an offence for any person to call upon an African to defy. Contravention of this proclamation carried a penalty of three years or of a fine of three hundred pounds. In March this year the Government passed the so-called Public Safety Act which empowered it to declare a state of emergency and to create conditions which would permit of the most ruthless and pitiless methods of suppressing our movement. Almost simultaneously, the Criminal Laws Amendment Act was passed which provided heavy penalties for those convicted of Defiance offences. This Act also made provision for the whipping of defiers including women. It was under this Act that Mr. Arthur Matlala who was the local leader of the Central Branch during the Defiance Campaign, was convicted and sentenced to twelve months with hard labour plus eight strokes by the Magistrate of Villa Nora. The Government also made extensive use of the Suppression of Communism Act. You will remember that in May last year the Government ordered Moses Kotane, Yusuf Dadoo, J. B. Marks, David Bopape and Johnson Ngwevela to resign from the Congresses and many other organisations and were also prohibited from attending political gatherings. In consequence of these bans, Moses Kotane, J. B. Marks, and David Bopape did not attend our last provincial Conference. In December last year, the Secretary General, Mr. W. M. Sisulu, and I were banned from attending gatherings and confined to

Johannesburg for six months. Early this year, the President-General, Chief Luthuli, whilst in the midst of a national tour which he was prosecuting with remarkable energy and devotion, was prohibited for a period of twelve months from attending public gatherings and from visiting Durban, Johannesburg, Cape Town, Port Elizabeth and many other centres. A few days before the President-General was banned, the President of the SAIC, Dr. G. M. Naicker, had been served with a similar notice. Many other active workers both from the African and Indian Congresses and from trade union organisations were also banned.

The Congresses realised that these measures created a new situation which did not prevail when the Campaign was launched in June 1952. The tide of defiance was bound to recede and we were forced to pause and to take stock of the new situation. We had to analyse the dangers that faced us, formulate plans to overcome them and evolve new plans of political struggle. A political movement must keep in touch with reality and the prevailing conditions. Long speeches, the shaking of fists, the banging of tables and strongly worded resolutions out of touch with the objective conditions do not bring about mass action and can do a great deal of harm to the organisation and the struggle we serve. The masses had to be prepared and made ready for new forms of political struggle. We had to recuperate our strength and muster our forces for another and more powerful offensive against the enemy. To have gone ahead blindly as if nothing had happened would have been suicidal and stupid. The conditions under which we meet today are, therefore, vastly different. The Defiance Campaign together with its thrills and adventures has receded. The old methods of bringing about mass action through public mass meetings, press statements and leaflets calling upon the people to go to action have become extremely dangerous and difficult to use effectively. The authorities will not easily permit a meeting called under the auspices of the ANC, few newspapers will publish statements openly criticising the policies of the Government, and there is hardly a single printing press which will agree to print leaflets calling upon workers to embark on industrial action for fear of prosecution under the Suppression of Communism Act and similar measures. These developments require the evolution of new forms of political struggle which will make it reasonable for us to strive for action on a higher level than the Defiance Campaign. The Government, alarmed at the indomitable upsurge of national consciousness, is doing everything in its power to crush our movement by removing the genuine representatives of the people from the organisations. According to a statement made by Swart in Parliament on the 18th September, 1953, there are thirty-three trade union officials and eighty-nine other people who have been served with notices in terms of the Suppression of Communism Act. This does not include that formidable array of freedom fighters who have been named and blacklisted under the Suppression of Communism Act and those who have been banned under the Riotous Assemblies Act.

Meanwhile the living conditions of the people, already extremely difficult, are steadily worsening and becoming unbearable. The purchasing power of the masses is progressively declining and the cost of living is rocketing. Bread is now dearer than it was two months ago. The cost of milk, meat and vegetables is beyond the pockets of the average family and many of our people cannot afford them. The people are too poor to have enough food to feed their families and children. They cannot afford sufficient clothing, housing and medical care. They are denied the right to security in the event of unemployment, sickness, disability, old age; and where these exist, they are of an extremely inferior and useless nature. Because of lack of proper medical amenities our people are ravaged by such dreaded diseases as tuberculosis, venereal disease, leprosy, pellagra; and infantile mortality is very high. The recent state budget made provision for the increase of the cost-of-living allowances for Europeans and not a word was said about the poorest and most hard-hit section of the population — the African people. The insane policies of the Government which have brought about an explosive situation in the country have definitely scared away foreign capital from South Africa and the financial crisis through which the country is now passing is forcing many industrial and business concerns to close down, to retrench their staffs, and unemployment is growing every day. The farm labourers are in a particularly dire plight. You will perhaps recall the investigations and exposures of the semi-slave conditions on the Bethal farms made in 1948 by the Reverend Michael Scott and a *Guardian* correspondent; by the *Drum* last year and the *Advance* in April this year. You will recall how human beings, wearing only sacks with holes for their heads and arms, never given enough food to eat, slept on cement floors on cold nights with only their sacks to cover their shivering bodies. You will remember how they are woken up as early as 4 a. m. and taken to work on the fields with the indunas sjambokking those who tried to straighten their backs, who felt weak and dropped down because of hunger and sheer exhaustion. You will also recall the story of human beings toiling pathetically from the early hours of the morning till sunset, fed only on mealie meal served on filthy sacks spread on the ground and eating with their dirty hands. People falling ill and never once being given medical attention. You will also recall the revolting story of a farmer who was convicted for tying a labourer by his feet from a tree and had him flogged to death, pouring boiling water into his mouth whenever he cried for water. These things which have long vanished from many parts of the world still flourish in SA today. None will deny that they constitute a serious challenge to Congress and we are in duty bound to find an effective remedy for these obnoxious practices.

The Government has introduced in Parliament the Native Labour (Settlement of Disputes) Bill and the Bantu Education Bill. Speaking on the Labour Bill, the Minister of Labour, Ben Schoeman, openly stated that the aim of this wicked measure is to bleed African trade unions to death. By forbidding strikes and lockouts it deprives Africans of the one weapon the workers have to improve their position. The aim of the measure is to destroy the present African trade unions, which are controlled by the workers themselves and which fight for the improvement of their working conditions, in return for a Central Native Labour Board controlled by the Government and which will be used to frustrate the legitimate aspirations of the African worker. The Minister of Native Affairs, Verwoerd, has also been brutally clear in explaining the objects of the Bantu Education Bill. According to him the aim of this law is to teach our children that Africans are inferior to Europeans. African education would be taken out of the hands of people who taught equality between black and white. When this Bill becomes law, it will not be the parents but the Department of Native Affairs which will decide whether an African child should receive higher or other education. It might well be that the children of those who criticise the Government and who fight its policies will almost certainly be taught how to drill rocks in the mines and how to plough potatoes on the farms of Bethal. High education might well be the privilege of those children whose families have a tradition of collaboration with the ruling circles.

The attitude of the Congress on these bills is very clear and unequivocal. Congress totally rejects both bills without reservation. The last provincial Conference strongly condemned the then proposed Labour Bill as a measure designed to rob the African workers of the universal right of free trade unionism and to undermine and destroy the existing African trade unions. Conference further called upon the African workers to boycott and defy the application of this sinister scheme which was calculated to further the exploitation of the African worker. To accept a measure of this nature even in a qualified manner would be a betrayal of the toiling masses. At a time when every genuine Congressite should fight unreservedly for the recognition of African trade unions and the realisation of the principle that everyone has the right to form and to join trade unions for the protection of his interests, we declare our firm belief in the principles enunciated in the Universal Declaration of Human Rights that everyone has the right to education; that education shall be directed to the full development of human personality and to the strengthening of respect for human rights and fundamental freedoms. It shall promote understanding, tolerance and friendship among the nations, racial or religious groups and shall further the activities of the United Nations for the maintenance of peace. That parents have the right to choose the kind of education that shall be given to their children.

The cumulative effect of all these measures is to prop up and perpetuate the artificial and decaying policy of the supremacy of the white men. The attitude of the government to us is that: "Let's beat them down with guns and batons and trample them under our feet. We must be ready to drown the whole country in blood if only there is the slightest chance of preserving white supremacy."

But there is nothing inherently superior about the *herrenvolk* idea of the supremacy of the whites. In China, India, Indonesia and Korea, American, British, Dutch and French Imperialism, based on the concept of the supremacy of Europeans over Asians, has been completely and perfectly exploded. In Malaya and Indo-China British and French imperialisms are being shaken to their foundations by powerful and revolutionary national liberation movements. In Africa, there are approximately 190,000,000 Africans as against 4,000,000 Europeans. The entire continent is seething with discontent and already there are powerful revolutionary eruptions in the Gold Coast, Nigeria, Tunisia, Kenya, the Rhodesias and South Africa. The oppressed people and the oppressors are at loggerheads. The *day of reckoning* between the forces of freedom and those of reaction is not very far off. I have not the slightest doubt that when that day comes truth and justice will prevail.

The intensification of repressions and the extensive use of the bans is designed to immobilise every active worker and to check the national liberation movement. But gone forever are the days when harsh and wicked laws provided the oppressors with years of peace and quiet. The racial policies of the Government have pricked the conscience of all men of good will and have aroused their deepest indignation. The feelings of the oppressed people have never been more bitter. If the ruling circles seek to maintain their position by such inhuman methods then a clash between the forces of freedom and those of reaction is certain. The grave plight of the people compels them to resist to the death the stinking policies of the gangsters that rule our country.

But in spite of all the difficulties outlined above, we have won important victories. The general political level of the people has been considerably raised and they are now more conscious of their strength. Action has become the language of the day. The ties between the working people and the Congress have been greatly strengthened. This is a development of the highest importance because in a country such as ours a political organisation that does not receive the support of the workers is in fact paralysed on the very ground on which it has chosen to wage battle. Leaders of trade union organisations are at the same time important officials of the provincial and local branches of the ANC. In the past we talked of the African, Indian and Coloured struggles. Though certain individuals raised the question of a united front of all the oppressed groups, the various non-European organisations stood miles apart from one another and the efforts of those for co-ordination and unity were like a voice crying in the wilderness, and it seemed that the day would never dawn when the oppressed people would stand and fight together shoulder to shoulder against a common enemy. Today we talk of the struggle of the oppressed people which, though it is waged through their respective autonomous organisations, is gravitating towards one central command.

Our immediate task is to consolidate these victories, to preserve our organisations and to muster our forces for the resumption of the offensive. To achieve this important task the National Executive of the ANC in consultation with the National Action Committee of the ANC and the SAIC formulated a plan of action popularly known as the "M" Plan and the highest importance is given to it by the National

Executives. Instructions were given to all provinces to implement the "M" Plan without delay.

The underlying principle of this plan is the understanding that it is no longer possible to wage our struggle mainly on the old methods of public meetings and printed circulars. The aim is:

to consolidate the Congress machinery;

to enable the transmission of important decisions taken on a national level to every member of the organisation without calling public meetings, issuing press statements and printing circulars;

to build up in the local branches themselves local Congresses which will effectively represent the strength and will of the people;

to extend and strengthen the ties between Congress and the people and to consolidate Congress leadership.

This plan is being implemented in many branches not only in the Transvaal but also in the other provinces and is producing excellent results. The Regional Conferences held in Sophiatown, Germiston, Kliptown and Benoni on the 28th June, 23rd and 30th August and on the 6th September, 1953, which were attended by large crowds, are a striking demonstration of the effectiveness of this plan, and the National Executives must be complimented for it. I appeal to all members of the Congress to redouble their efforts and play their part truly and well in its implementation. The hard, dirty and strenuous task of recruiting members and strengthening our organisation through a house to house campaign in every locality must be done by you all. From now on the activity of Congressites must not be confined to speeches and resolutions. Their activities must find expression in wide scale work among the masses, work which will enable them to make the greatest possible contact with the working people. You must protect and defend your trade unions. If you are not allowed to have your meetings publicly, then you must hold them over your machines in the factories, on the trains and buses as you travel home. You must have them in your villages and shantytowns. You must make every home, every shack and every mud structure where our people live, a branch of the trade union movement, and never surrender.

You must defend the right of African parents to decide the kind of education that shall be given to their children. Teach the children that Africans are not one iota inferior to Europeans. Establish your own community schools where the right kind of education will be given to our children. If it becomes dangerous or impossible to have these alternative schools, then again you must make every home, every shack or rickety structure a centre of learning for our children. Never surrender to the inhuman and barbaric theories of Verwoerd.

The decision to defy the unjust laws enabled Congress to develop considerably wider contacts between itself and the masses and the urge to join Congress grew day by day. But due to the fact that the local branches did not exercise proper control and supervision, the admission of new members was not carried out satisfactorily. No careful examination was made of their past history and political characteristics. As a result of this, there were many shady characters ranging from political clowns, place-seekers, splitters, saboteurs, agents-provocateurs, to informers and even policemen, who infiltrated into the ranks of Congress. One need only refer to the Johannesburg trial of Dr. Moroka and nineteen others, where a member of Congress who actually worked at the National Headquarters, turned out to be a detective-sergeant on special duty. Remember the case of Leballo of Brakpan who wormed himself into that Branch by producing faked naming letters from the Liquidator, De Villiers Louw, who had instructions to spy on us. There are many other similar instances that emerged during the Johannesburg, Port Elizabeth and Kimberley trials. Whilst some of these men were discovered there are many who have not been found out. In Congress there are still many shady characters, political clowns, place-seekers, saboteurs, provocateurs, informers and policemen who masquerade as progressives but who are in fact the bitterest enemies of our organisation. Outside appearances are highly deceptive and we cannot classify these men by looking at their faces or by listening to their sweet tongues or their vehement speeches demanding immediate action. The friends of the people are distinguishable by the ready and disciplined manner in which they rally behind their organisation and their readiness to sacrifice when the preservation of the organisation has become a matter of life and death. Similarly, enemies and shady characters are detected by the extent to which they consistently attempt to wreck the organisation by creating fratricidal strife, disseminating confusion and undermining and even opposing important plans of action to vitalise the organisation.

In this respect it is interesting to note that almost all the people who oppose the "M" Plan are people who have consistently refused to respond when sacrifices were called for, and whose political background leaves much to be desired. These shady characters by means of flattery, bribes and corruption, win the support of the weak-willed and politically backward individuals, detach them from Congress and use them in their own interests. The presence of such elements in Congress constitutes a serious threat to the struggle, for the capacity for political action of an organisation which is ravaged by such disruptive and splitting elements is considerably undermined. Here in South Africa, as in many parts of the world, a revolution is maturing: it is the profound desire, the determination and the urge of the overwhelming majority of the country to destroy forever the shackles of oppression that condemn them to servitude and slavery. To overthrow oppression has been sanctioned by humanity and is the highest aspiration of every free man. If elements in our organisation seek to impede the realisation of this lofty purpose then these people have placed themselves outside the organisation and must be put out of action before they do more harm. To do otherwise would be a crime and a serious neglect of duty. We must rid ourselves of such elements and give our organisation the striking power of a real militant mass organisation.

Kotane, Marks, Bopape, Tloome and I have been banned from attending gatherings and we cannot join and counsel with you on the serious problems that are facing our country. We have been banned because we champion the freedom of the oppressed people of our country and because we have consistently fought against the policy of racial discrimination in favour of a policy which accords fundamental human rights to all, irrespective of race, colour, sex or language. We are exiled from our own people, for we have uncompromisingly resisted the efforts of imperialist America and her satellites to drag the world into the rule of violence and brutal force, into the rule of the napalm, hydrogen and the cobalt bombs, where millions of people will be wiped out to satisfy the criminal and greedy appetites of the imperial powers. We have been gagged because we have emphatically and openly condemned the criminal attacks by the imperialists against the people of Malaya, Vietnam, Indonesia, Tunisia and Tanganyika and called upon our people to identify themselves unreservedly with the cause of world peace and to fight against the war policies of America and her satellites. We are being shadowed, hounded and trailed because we fearlessly voiced our horror and indignation at the slaughter of the people of Korea and Kenya. The massacre of the Kenya people by Britain has aroused world-wide indignation and protest. Children are being burnt alive, women are raped, tortured, whipped and boiling water poured on their breasts to force confessions from them that Jomo Kenyatta had administered the Mau Mau oath to them. Men are being castrated and shot dead. In the Kikuyu country there are some villages in which the population has been completely wiped out. We are prisoners in our own country because we dared to raise our voices against these horrible atrocities and because we expressed our solidarity with the cause of the Kenya people.

You can see that "there is no easy walk to freedom anywhere, and many of us will have to pass through the valley of the shadow (of death) again and again before we reach the mountain tops of our desires."

"Dangers and difficulties have not deterred us in the past, they will not frighten us now. But we must be prepared for them like men in business who do not waste energy in vain talk and idle action. The way of preparation (for action) lies in our rooting out all impurity and indiscipline from our organisation and making it the bright and shining instrument that will cleave its way to (Africa's) freedom."

General Strike

June 1961

The call of the All-in African National Action Council for a stay-at-home on 29, 30 and 31 May 1961 received solid and massive support throughout the country. This magnificent response was the result of the hard work and selfless devotion of our organisers and activists who had to overcome formidable difficulties, very often involving personal risks to themselves. Defying unprecedented intimidation by the State, trailed and hounded by the Special Branch, denied the right to hold meetings, operating in areas heavily patrolled by government and municipal police and teeming with spies and informers, they stood firm as a rock and spread the stay-at-home message to millions of people throughout the country. Ever since the All-in African Conference at Pietermaritzburg, the issue that dominated South African politics and that attracted pressmen from all over the world was not the Republican celebrations organised by the government, but the stirring campaign of the African people and other non-White sections to mark our rejection of a White Republic forcibly imposed upon us by a minority.

Few political organisations could have succeeded in conducting such a stubborn and relentless campaign under conditions which, for all practical purposes, amounted to martial law. But we did so. The steps taken by the government to suppress the campaign were a measure of our strength and influence in the political life of the country and of its weakness. The government was alarmed by the tremendous impact of the demand for a national convention and the call for countrywide anti-Republican demonstrations. It realised that there would be overwhelming support for the call if the campaign was not immediately suppressed through open terror and intimidation. It also realised that the organisational machine built up to propagate the campaign was of so high a standard, and support for the idea so firm and widespread, that the situation could only be controlled by resorting to naked force. Only by mobilising the entire resources of the State could the government hope to stem the tide that was running so strongly against it.

A special law had to be rushed through parliament to enable the government to detain without trial people connected with the organisation of the stay-at-home. The army had to be called out, European civilians armed, and the police force deployed in African townships and other areas. Meetings were banned throughout the country, and the local authorities, in collaboration with the police-force, kept vigil to ensure that no strike propaganda should be spread amongst the masses of the people. More than ten thousand innocent Africans were arrested and jailed under the pass laws, and terror and intimidation became widespread. Only by adopting these strong-arm measures could the government hope to break the stay-at-home. By resorting to these drastic steps the government has in fact conceded that we are the country's most powerful and dangerous opponents to its hated policies.

On this issue, the radio, the press, and European employers played a thoroughly shameful role. At the beginning of the campaign the press gave us fairly objective coverage and, acting on information supplied by their own reporters in different parts of the country, they reported growing support for the demonstrations and correctly predicted unprecedented response to the call. Until a week or so before the stay-at-home, the South African press endeavoured to live up to the standards and ethics of honest journalism and reported news items as they were without slants and distortions. But as soon as the government showed the mailed fist and threatened action against those newspapers that gave publicity to the campaign, the Opposition press, true to tradition, beat a hurried retreat and threw all principles and ethical standards overboard.

On 18 May 1961, the Johannesburg *Rand Daily Mail* published a front-page news item alleging that the National Action Council had secret plans to bring thousands of non-whites into the central areas of cities. It also announced that the NAC had held a secret meeting the week before at which it decided to extend the duration of the stay-at-home beyond the three-day period. According to the same report, the announcement of the extension of the period would be made at the last moment to retain the element of surprise. In a front-page leading article of the same issue of this newspaper, its editor stated that he and the police possessed information that some of us planned violent disturbances on the eve of the Republic.

On behalf of the NAC I immediately replied in writing and refuted all the allegations contained in the news item as sensational journalism and as the inventions of an over-enthusiastic reporter who had sucked things out of his thumbs. We reiterated that this particular campaign was planned to be disciplined and non-violent and that we had no intention whatsoever of exposing our unarmed people to situations whereby they could become targets for the trigger-happy police. In regard to the leading article, we agreed that violence was an unfortunate thing. We felt, however, that appeals for non-violence should be addressed to the government, who were spoiling for a showdown and massacre, and not to the African people, who had repeatedly protested the peaceful and non-violent character of their campaign. We also felt it to be our duty to place on record that, if people in history had listened to appeals to drop political campaigns launched to back up the demands of an oppressed people simply because violence might occur in the course of such a campaign, the world today would still be languishing under the despotic rule of the Middle Ages. Although honour and duty obliged him to publish my reply the editor deliberately decided to suppress it. I spoke to him twice thereafter and, although he promised to attend to the matter, the reply never saw the light of day. We suspected that more was involved than met the eye.

In the evening of 29 May 1961, I made a statement to the same newspaper. I pointed out that in the light of the conditions that prevailed then, the response to the call of the NAC had been solid and substantial and that hundreds of thousands of our people had stayed away from work. I pointed out, however, that the overall response had fallen short of expectations and that we had, consequently, given instructions to our regional and local Action Committees throughout the country to swing into action and to work hard during the night to ensure greater success the following day. This statement was distorted to give the impression that we had conceded defeat and, in this distorted form, it was distributed by the *Rand Daily Mail* to other morning newspapers throughout the country—a deliberate act of sabotage.

This sudden somersault was not confined to the *Rand Daily Mail* only. With the exception of *Contact, Post, New Age, Drum*, the *World* and a few other newspapers, the Opposition press changed suddenly and simultaneously.

Undue prominence was given to statements made by government leaders, mayors of cities, managers of Non-European Affairs departments, and by employers' organisations, in which the stay-at-home was condemned and appeals made to workers to ignore the call. Statements made by the NAC were either distorted, watered down, or even suppressed deliberately. For example, on 20 May 1961 the NAC issued a press statement strongly protesting at the unwarranted arrest of more than ten thousand innocent Africans. We condemned this police action as a blatant persecution of our voteless people by a European minority which we could no longer tolerate. We placed on record that we were deeply incensed by this provocative action and demanded the immediate stopping of the arrests and the unconditional release of all those detained. Not a single Opposition newspaper published this statement, notwithstanding the extensive publicity they gave this police operation and the unwarranted compliment they paid to the same police for the courteous manner in which they were alleged to have carried out the operation. These arrests were made for the purpose of forestalling demonstrations planned by us. We had gone through numerous road blocks in various parts of the country, and it was our people who had been rounded up under a system which is rejected by the entire African nation, and which has been condemned by every government commission which considered it. Was it not important for the country to know what our views were on a matter of such importance?

The press was even more treacherous on the morning of the first day of the stay-at-home. The deliberate falsehoods spread by the police and radio were reproduced. At seven o'clock in the morning of that day, Radio South Africa broadcast news that workers throughout the country had ignored the call for a stay-at-home. The country was told that this news was based on statements made at six o'clock the same morning by Colonel Spengler, head of the Witwatersrand branch of the Special Branch. Similar statements made at approximately the same time by other police officers in different parts of the country were quoted. This means that long before the factory gates were opened and, in some areas, even before the workers boarded their trains and buses to work, the police had already announced that the stay-at-home had collapsed. I cannot imagine anything more fraudulent.

The *Rand Daily Mail* issued a special edition in which it almost echoed police reports. But the truth could not be suppressed for long. The Johannesburg *Star* of the same day reported that "Early estimates of absenteeism in Johannesburg ranged from 40 per cent to 75 per cent." This admission was only a small portion of the truth. As the days rolled by, news came through that hundreds of thousands of workers and students throughout the country had given massive support to the call. On 3 June 1961, *Post*, a Johannesburg Sunday newspaper with a huge circulation, published reports from its team of crack reporters and photographers who had kept a continuous watch on townships in different parts of South Africa and who conducted detailed personal investigations inside and outside of these areas. Said the newspaper: "Many thousands of workers registered their protest against the Republic and the Government's refusal to cooperate with non-Whites. *They did not go to work.* They disrupted much of South African commerce and industry. Some factories worked with skeleton staffs, others closed, and many other businesses were shut down for the three days." The leading article of the *New Age* of 8 June 1961 acclaimed the stay-at-home as the most widespread general strike on a national scale that this country had ever seen.

Contact of 1 June 1961 wrote: "On Tuesday 50 per cent of Indian workers in Durban were still out. Some factories showed 100 per cent success with some clothing factories 100 per cent unattended. In Durban and Pietermaritzburg most Indian businesses were closed on Monday and open again on Tuesday. Large numbers of schoolchildren kept away from school. There were attacks on buses at Cato Manor and a bus to Pietermaritzburg from a Reserve was fired on." Sam Sly, writing in the same paper on 15 June 1961, observed: "In defiance of that sickening and sterile rule, there were plenty of politics on plenty of campuses. Enough to bring large bands of armed police to five campuses. There was defiance, leadership, and courage amongst the students. There was political awareness, even non-racial solidarity. Before, what had one heard but minority protests lost among the sounds of the inter-varsity rugby crowd or the chatter in the students' cafeteria."

A Port Elizabeth daily newspaper estimated that about 75 per cent of that city's non-White population stayed away on 30 May 1961.

The truth had come out. From various parts of the country news came through testifying to widespread support for the call.

Students at the University College of Fort Hare, at Healdtown and Lovedale all stayed away from classes. At the University of Natal, which has about five hundred non-White students, less than fifty attended classes. Throughout the country thousands of students in primary and secondary schools stayed away from classes and boycotted republican celebrations. The Transkeian Territories have been under martial law for many months now. The barbarous and cruel policies of the Nationalist Government find expression in extremely savage attacks on the innocent and unarmed people of these areas. Many have been murdered by the government and their stooges, thousands have been beaten up and injured, uprooted and driven away from their lands and homes. Hundreds of freedom fighters are languishing in jails for demanding freedom and justice for the people of the Transkei. Even in this area of death and hell, the flames of freedom are scorching meadows. Umtata, the capital of the area, bore witness to this fact the other day. Students of St John's College, in a militant and inspiring demonstration, showed that the days of despots and tyrants are numbered.

A detailed survey conducted by the South African Congress of Trade Unions shows that in Johannesburg, Durban, Port Elizabeth, Cape Town and other centres, the clothing, textile, laundry and dry-cleaning, food and canning, and furniture industries were severely hit.

In the light of the conditions that prevailed both before and during the three-day strike, the response from our people was magnificent indeed. The failure of the government, the employers, and the press to break us down pays tribute to the matchless courage and determination of our people, and to the skilful and speedy manner in which our organisational machine was able to adapt itself to new conditions, new obstacles, new dangers.

The stay-at-home was also opposed by former members of the Pan-Africanist Congress (PAC), the Society of Young Africa and the Sons of Zululand. The name of Peter Makhene was also mentioned. He was described as leader of the Bantu National Congress and claimed a membership of fifty thousand. The newspaper that published his statement made it clear that this gentleman is a supporter of the government and its policies. It is, therefore, part of his functions to sell apartheid to Africans. He is compelled to oppose all political organisations which fight for the defeat of the Verwoerd fascist republic. But what we want to know is where and when was this organisation established. Has it any constitution? Who are its officials? Has it had any conferences or meetings? If so, when and where? People will be excused if they feel that this organisation went underground long before it was established. It simply does not exist.

The Sons of Zululand and the Society of Young Africa are not genuine organisations but cliques and sects which are completely unknown to Africans and which have never had any following whatsoever amongst our people.

The Society of Young Africa (or SOYA), like its parent body the Unity Movement from which it broke away a few years ago, is an insignificant sect of bitter and frustrated intellectuals who have completely lost confidence in themselves, who have no political ambitions whatsoever and who abhor serious political struggle. In the whole history of their existence they have never found it possible to rise above the level of saboteurs and scandal mongers. Together with the Peter Makhenes and the Sons of

Zululand they invariably disappear from the political scene and suddenly come to light fighting side by side with the police to oppose the just struggles of the African people. Africans know who their friends and enemies are and these cliques are treated throughout the country with the contempt they deserve. No useful purpose will be served by wasting more ink and paper on bogus organisations which, under the pretext of ultra-revolutionary language, permit themselves to be used by the police against the struggles of their kith and kin.

The attitude of former members of the PAC on the stay-at-home has been one of shocking contradiction and amazing confusion. Nothing has been more disastrous to themselves than their pathetic attempts to sabotage the demonstrations.

First, they attended the Consultative Conference of African leaders held in Orlando in December 1960 as delegates, took part in the deliberations and fully supported the resolution adopted at that conference calling for unity amongst Africans and for a multi-racial national convention. At this conference a Continuation Committee was elected to prepare for the All-in African Conference which was subsequently held at Pietermaritzburg. Their representative served on this committee for several months with full knowledge that its main function was to unite all Africans on an anti-Republican front and for a sovereign convention of all South Africans to draw up a new democratic constitution for the country. Towards the end of February this year, and without so much as a hint to their colleagues on the Continuation Committee, they issued a press statement announcing that they would not take part in the Pietermaritzburg talks. Their failure to raise the matter in the committee before they withdrew betrays the underhand and traitorous nature of this manoeuvre and indicates that they well knew that they could find no political justification whatsoever for their action.

Secondly, there was a sharp conflict between former leaders of the PAC on the South African United Front overseas, and the local leaders. Whilst the latter opposed, the former gave support. A message from Dar-es-Salaam, signed by J J Hadebe and Gaur Radebe, former members of the ANC and PAC respectively, said:

"The South African United Front congratulates the Continuation Committee of the people's conference held at Pietermaritzburg for organising demonstrations on the eve of the South African Republic which threatens to further oppress and persecute the people."

Even locally there were many former PAC people who bitterly disagreed with their leaders and who felt that they could not follow the stupid and disastrous blunders they were advocating.

But there was something even more disastrous and tragic than their mean and cowardly behaviour in stabbing their kith and kin at a time when maximum unity had become a matter of life and death to Africans. What shocked most people was the extent to which they completely identified themselves with the action of the police in the repression of the demonstrations. We have already indicated the unprecedented measures adopted by the government to deal with our campaign. These measures provoked strong protests from many organisations and individuals, but there was not a single word of protest from the former PAC people. Why? Precisely because their main function was to ruin African unity and to break the strike. To protest against these savage onslaughts on the African people would have been an unfriendly act to the government with whom they were now allied. They purchased collaboration with the government as the price of turning a deaf ear to the sufferings of the African people.

Authentic reports from different parts of the country revealed that the police did not interfere with the distribution of PAC leaflets and, in some areas, members of the police force even distributed leaflets purporting to have been issued by the PAC and attacking the strike.

This collaboration was not confined to negative acts of passivity. In its positive form it expressed itself in desperate attempts both by the police and the PAC people to track down the people behind the campaign. For security reasons, the identity of members of the NAC was kept a closely guarded secret. The police conducted extensive investigations to find this information in order to arrest members of this body. At the same time the PAC people called on us to publish the information and protested that we had to communicate with the press from public telephone booths. Why were they interested in this information? They knew all the members of the Continuation Committee. They withdrew from that committee and from the campaign not because they did not know its members but in spite of that knowledge. Such information was useless to them because they were out of the campaign but extremely useful to the police. On which side of the fence are these people? What sort of political organisation is this that deliberately sets traps for leaders of another political body? Who are they trying to bluff by pretending that they are still against the government and fighting for the welfare of the African people?

Differences between rival political organisations in the liberation camp on tactical questions are permissible. But for a political body which purports to be part of the liberation struggle to pursue a line which objectively supports a government that suppresses Africans is treacherous and unforgivable. We called on the African people to reject the Verwoerd republic not because we preferred a monarchical form of government, but because we felt that the introduction of a republic should only take place after seeking the views and after obtaining the express consent of the African people. We felt that the foundations of the republic, as of the State that existed prior to the proclamation of the republic, would be based on apartheid and the exploitation of the African people. The government rejected our demands, called upon the African people to ignore our call and to participate fully in the republican celebrations and to co-operate with the new government. The Africanists echoed the government by asking Africans to ignore the call but deliberately elected to remain silent on the vital question whether or not they should co-operate with the republic. An ingenious way of saying that we should participate and co-operate.

A political organisation that is forced by opportunism and petty political rivalries into allying itself with the enemies of an oppressed community is doomed. The African people demand freedom and self-rule. They refuse to cooperate with the Verwoerd republic or with any government based upon force. PAC has ruined its future by opposing this dynamic demand. That is why most Africans, including many who once supported them, are so strong in condemning their treachery.

But all this discussion has now become academic because for all practical purposes the PAC has lost considerable support even in areas where only last year it achieved spectacular success. In February this year they announced plans to stage demonstrations from 21 March 1961. Leaflets were issued in Cape Town and were widely distributed in Langa and Nyanga African townships calling upon people to stock food and to prepare themselves for action on this date. In Johannesburg and Vereeniging stickers appeared here and there calling upon Africans to observe 21 March as the day of struggle. The whole thing fizzled out long before the much-heralded day, and when the date arrived not a single person responded either in Cape Town, Vereeniging, or Johannesburg. The episode was not regarded as sufficiently newsworthy even to be mentioned as a failure by the press either here or abroad. For the second time in two months they have suffered yet another defeat. Their efforts to sabotage the recent strike misfired badly. Hundreds of thousands of workers throughout the country, businessmen in town and country and thousands upon thousands of students in primary and secondary schools, treated the PAC with utter contempt and responded magnificently to our call. The results prove that no power on earth can stop an oppressed population determined to win its freedom. In the meantime, the PAC has been shocked and stunned by this rebuff and they sit licking their wounds, unable to look people in the face and haunted by the enormity of their outrageous crime.

One of the most significant factors about the stay-at-home was the wide support it received from students and the militant and stirring demonstrations it inspired amongst them. African students at Fort Hare, Natal University, Lovedale, Healdtown and in many other institutions throughout the country demonstrated their support for the call and stayed away from lectures. In primary and secondary schools throughout the country, scholars boycotted republican celebrations, refused commemoration medals, and stayed away from schools. There were militant and inspiring demonstrations at St John's College at Umtata and at the Botha Sigcau College in the Transkei. There were equally impressive ones in Kilnerton and Bloemfontein. This is an extremely significant development because students are the life-blood of a political movement and the upsurge of national consciousness amongst them spells death and destruction to those who oppose the claims and legitimate aspirations of the African people.

European students at the University of Rhodes, and at the Witwatersrand University, also played a prominent part in the demonstrations. Their support showed that even amongst the Whites the forces of challenge and opposition to White supremacy exist and are ready to join battle whenever the call is made.

On 1 June 1961, the NAC issued a press statement strongly condemning the victimisation of students who participated in the strike and demanded that the tyrannical orders for the closing of some of the colleges should be withdrawn and the colleges reopened at once. We congratulated the students for their public spirited action in which, as befits the intellectual youth, they gave a courageous lead to the nation at a time when courage and leadership were qualities we needed most. However much the authorities may try to play down the importance and significance of this development amongst the African youth, there can be no doubt that they realise that the writing is on the wall and that the days of White supremacy in our country are numbered.

The response of the Coloured people was equally impressive. They showed immense courage and militancy. In a country where they have always been treated as an appendage of the ruling White group and in which official policy had tended to treat them differently from the rest of the non-White population, it is significant and most heartening that they decided to make common cause with us by coming out clearly against the Verwoerd republic. This development marks a landmark in the political struggles of the non-Whites in this country.

The entire Indian community threw its powerful resources behind the campaign. Indian workers stayed away from work. Businessmen closed their businesses and students stayed away from schools and refused medals.

The forces of liberation are strong and powerful and their numbers are growing. The morale is high and we look forward to the future with perfect confidence.

It would, however, be a mistake to exaggerate our success. In spite of the magnificent courage shown by our people, numerical response fell below expectations. Mistakes were committed and weaknesses and shortcomings were discovered. They must be attended to. We must make adjustments in our methods and style of work to meet contingencies which we did not anticipate. Only in this way shall we build more strength and increase our striking power.

People expressed the view that the issue on which the people were asked to strike, namely, the demand for a national convention, lacked emotional appeal and was, in any event, too complicated an issue to arouse enthusiasm. Facts contradict this viewpoint. The success of the Pietermaritzburg conference and the deep and widespread support for the eve of the Republic demonstrations, testified to not only by our organisers and activists, but by the South African press, and the fact that hundreds of thousands of people stayed away from work notwithstanding fierce intimidation by the government and threats of dismissal by employers, indicate that this issue aroused the greatest enthusiasm. What reduced the scope and extent of what would have been an unprecedented response were the drastic measures taken by the government to suppress the strike, intimidation by employers, and the falsehoods spread by the radio and the press.

A closely related argument is that the demand for a national convention does not deal with bread-and-butter issues. Of course the African people want bread and butter. Is there anybody who does not? We demand higher wages and we want more and better food in our pantries. But we also need the vote to legislate decent laws. This is the importance of the demand for a national convention. One man, one vote, is the key to our future.

Another argument is that the strike was called by an ad hoc committee whose members were unknown to the public, that the voice of Chief A J Lutuli, the most powerful and popular leader of the African people, and that of the African National Congress, the sword and shield of the African people for the last fifty years, were never heard. The argument continues that the public may have doubted whether the African leaders were in fact behind the demonstration. In the first place, Chief Lutuli was a member of the Continuation Committee which organised the Pietermaritzburg conference, and he sent a dynamic message to that gathering which was loudly cheered. In the second place, the names of members of the NAC were, for obvious reasons, never published and the public may never know whether or not Chief Lutuli was a member. It would have been naive for us to have stood on the mountain tops and proclaimed that he was a member directing his forces as he has always done in previous campaigns. His courage and devotion to the cause of freedom is known in every household in this country. Inside and outside committees he remains the undisputed and most respected leader of the African people and a source of tremendous inspiration to all South African freedom fighters. He is a fearless opponent of the Nationalist government and leader of all the anti-Republican forces.

Of all the observations made on the strike, none has brought forth so much heat and emotion as the stress and emphasis we put on non-violence. Our most loyal supporters, whose courage and devotion has never been doubted, unanimously and strenuously disagreed with this approach and with the assurances we gave that we would not use any form of intimidation whatsoever to induce people to stay away from work. It was argued that the soil of our beloved country has been stained with the priceless blood of African patriots murdered by the Nationalist government in the course of peaceful and disciplined demonstrations to assert their claims and legitimate aspirations. It was the government that should have been told to refrain from its inhuman policy of violence and massacre, not the African people. It was further argued that it is wrong and indefensible for a political organisation to repudiate picketing, which is used the world over as a legitimate form of pressure to prevent scabbing.

Even up to the present day the question that is being asked with monotonous regularity up and down the country is this: is it politically correct to continue preaching peace and non-violence when dealing with a government whose barbaric practices have brought so much suffering and misery to Africans? With equal monotony the question is posed: have we not closed a chapter on this question? These are crucial questions that merit sane and sober reflection. It would be a serious mistake to brush them aside and leave them unanswered.

Numerous other observations were made by members of the public, by organisations and individuals, by sympathetic journals who have given us support and encouragement and by our own followers. All these have been noted. We appreciate that they were made in all humility with a view to better planning and more efficiency next time.

In rounding up this review we wish to congratulate once again all those patriotic workers, businessmen and students, black and white, who took part in this dynamic and historic demonstration and we compliment them most heartily for their courage in the face of fierce opposition and intimidation. This patriotism, this unity and this fearless spirit are the most precious investment this country has.

The strike at the end of May was only the beginning of our campaign. We are now launching a full-scale, countrywide campaign of non-cooperation with the Verwoerd government, until we have won an elected National Convention, representing all the people of this country, with the power to draw up and enforce a new democratic constitution.

Details of the campaign will be given from time to time. But let me say now that people without votes cannot be expected to go on paying taxes to a government of White domination. People who live in poverty cannot be expected to pay rents under threats of criminal prosecution and imprisonment. Above all, those who are oppressed cannot tolerate a situation where their own people man and maintain the machinery of their own national oppression. Africans cannot serve on school boards and school committees which are part of the Nationalists' Bantu Education. This is meant to deprive Africans of true education.

Only traitors can serve on tribal councils. These are a mockery of self government. They are meant to keep us forever in a state of slavery to Whites. We shall fight together tooth and nail, against the government plan to bring Bantu Authorities to the cities, just as our people in the rural areas have fought. Africans cannot continue to carry passes. Thousands of our people are sent away to jail every month under the pass laws.

We ask our millions of friends outside South Africa to intensify the boycott and isolation of the government of this country, diplomatically, economically, and in every other way.

The mines, industries, and farms of this country cannot carry on without the labour of Africans imported from elsewhere in Africa.

We are the people of this country. We produce the wealth of the gold mines, of the farms, and of industry. Non-collaboration is the weapon we must use to bring down the government. We have decided to use it fully and without reservation.

Black Man In A White Court

1962

MANDELA: Your Worship, before I plead to the charge, there are one or two points I would like to raise.

Firstly, Your Worship will recall that this matter was postponed last Monday at my request until today, to enable Counsel to make the arrangements to be available here today. Although Counsel is now available, after consultation with him and my attorneys, I have elected to conduct my own defence. Some time during the progress of these proceedings, I hope to be able to indicate that this case is a trial of the aspirations of the African people, and because of that I thought it proper to conduct my own defence. Nevertheless, I have decided to retain the services of Counsel, who will be here throughout these proceedings, and I also would like my attorney to be available in the course of these proceedings as well, but subject to that I will conduct my own defence.

The second point I would like to raise is an application which is addressed to Your Worship. Now at the outset, I want to make it perfectly clear that the remarks I am going to make are not addressed to Your Worship in his personal capacity, nor are they intended to reflect upon the integrity of the court. I hold Your Worship in high esteem and I do not for one single moment doubt your sense of fairness and justice. I must also mention that nothing I am going to raise in this application is intended to reflect against the Prosecutor in his personal capacity.

The point I wish to raise in my argument is based not on personal considerations, but on important questions that go beyond the scope of this present trial. I might also mention that in the course of this application I am frequently going to refer to the white man and the white people. I want at once to make it clear that I am no racialist, and I detest racialism, because I regard it as a barbaric thing, whether it comes from a black man or from a white man. The terminology that I am going to employ will be compelled on me by the nature of the application I am making.

I want to apply for Your Worship's recusal from this case. I challenge the right of this court to hear my case on two grounds.

Firstly, I challenge it because I fear that I will not be given a fair and proper trial. Secondly, I consider myself neither legally nor morally bound to obey laws made by a parliament in which I have no representation.

In a political trial such as this one, which involves a clash of the aspirations of the African people and those of whites, the country's courts, as presently constituted, cannot be impartial and fair.

In such cases, whites are interested parties. To have a white judicial officer presiding, however high his esteem, and however strong his sense of fairness and justice, is to make whites judges in their own case.

It is improper and against the elementary principles of justice to entrust whites with cases involving the denial by them of basic human rights to the African people.

What sort of justice is this that enables the aggrieved to sit in judgment over those against whom they have laid a charge?

A judiciary controlled entirely by whites and enforcing laws enacted by a white parliament in which Africans have no representation—laws which in most cases are passed in the face of unanimous opposition from Africans—

MAGISTRATE: I am wondering whether I shouldn't interfere with you at this stage, Mr Mandela. Aren't we going beyond the scope of the proceedings? After all is said and done, there is only one court today and that is the White Man's court. There is no other court. What purpose does it serve you to make an application when there is only one court, as you know yourself. What court do you wish to be tried by?

MANDELA: Well, Your Worship, firstly I would like Your Worship to bear in mind that in a series of cases our courts have laid it down that the right of a litigant to ask for a recusal of a judicial officer is an extremely important right, which must be given full protection by the court, as long as that right is exercised honestly. Now I honestly have apprehensions, as I am going to demonstrate just now, that this unfair discrimination throughout my life has been responsible for very grave injustices, and I am going to contend that that race discrimination which outside this court has been responsible for all my troubles, I fear in this court is going to do me the same injustice. Now Your Worship may disagree with that, but Your Worship is perfectly entitled, in fact, obliged to listen to me and because of that I feel that Your Worship-

MAGISTRATE: I would like to listen, but I would like you to give me the grounds for your application for me to recuse myself.

MANDELA: Well, these are the grounds, I am developing them, sir. If Your Worship will give me time—

MAGISTRATE: I don't wish to go out of the scope of the proceedings.

MANDELA:—Of the scope of the application. I am within the scope of the application, because I am putting forward grounds which in my opinion are likely not to give me a fair and proper trial.

MAGISTRATE: Anyway proceed.

MANDELA: As your Worship pleases. I was developing the point that a judiciary controlled entirely by whites and enforcing laws enacted by a white parliament in which we have no representation, laws which in most cases are passed in the face of unanimous opposition from Africans, cannot be regarded as an impartial tribunal in a political trial where an African stands as an accused.

The Universal Declaration of Human Rights provides that all men are equal before the law, and are entitled without any discrimination to equal protection of the law. In May 1951, Dr D F Malan, then Prime Minister, told the Union parliament that this provision of the Declaration applies in this country. Similar statements have been made on numerous occasions in the past by prominent whites in this country, including judges and magistrates. But the real truth is that there is in fact no equality before the law whatsoever as far as our people are concerned, and statements to the contrary are definitely incorrect and misleading.

It is true that an African who is charged in a court of law enjoys, on the surface, the same rights and privileges as an accused who is white in so far as the conduct of this trial is concerned. He is governed by the same rules of procedure and evidence as apply to a white accused. But it would be grossly inaccurate to conclude from this fact that an African consequently enjoys equality before the law.

In its proper meaning equality before the law means the right to participate in the making of the laws by which one is governed, a constitution which guarantees democratic rights to all sections of the population, the right to approach the court for protection or relief in the case of the violation of rights guaranteed in the constitution, and the right to take part in the administration of justice as judges, magistrates, attorneys-general, law advisers and similar positions.

In the absence of these safeguards the phrase "equality before the law", in so far as it is intended to apply to us, is meaningless and misleading. All the rights and privileges to which I have referred are monopolised by whites, and we enjoy none of them.

The white man makes all the laws, he drags us before his courts and accuses us, and he sits in judgment over us.

It is fit and proper to raise the question sharply, what is this rigid colour-bar in the administration of justice? Why is it that in this courtroom I face a white magistrate, am confronted by a white prosecutor, and escorted into the dock by a white orderly? Can anyone honestly and seriously suggest that in this type of atmosphere the scales of justice are evenly balanced?

Why is it that no African in the history of this country has ever had the honour of being tried by his own kith and kin, by his own flesh and blood?

I will tell Your Worship why: the real purpose of this rigid colour-bar is to ensure that the justice dispensed by the courts should conform to the policy of the country, however much that policy might be in conflict with the norms of justice accepted in judiciaries throughout the civilised world.

I feel oppressed by the atmosphere of white domination that lurks all around in this courtroom. Somehow this atmosphere calls to mind the inhuman injustices caused to my people outside this courtroom by this same white domination.

It reminds me that I am voteless because there is a parliament in this country that is white-controlled. I am without land because the white minority has taken a lion's share of my country and forced me to occupy poverty-stricken Reserves, over-populated and over-stocked. We are ravaged by starvation and disease . . .

MAGISTRATE: What has that got to do with the case, Mr. Mandela?

MANDELA: With the last point, Sir, it hangs together, if Your Worship will give me the chance to develop it.

MAGISTRATE: You have been developing it for quite a while now, and I feel you are going beyond the scope of your application.

MANDELA: Your Worship, this to me is an extremely important ground which the court must consider.

MAGISTRATE: I fully realise your position, Mr Mandela, but you must confine yourself to the application and not go beyond it. I don't want to know about starvation. That in my view has got nothing to do with the case at the present moment.

MANDELA: Well, Your Worship has already raised the point that here in this country there is only a white court. What is the point of all this? Now if I can demonstrate to Your Worship that outside this courtroom race discrimination has been used in such a way as to deprive me of my rights, not to treat me fairly, certainly this is a relevant fact from which to infer that wherever race discrimination is practised, this will be the same result, and this is the only reason why I am using this point.

MAGISTRATE: I am afraid that I will have to interrupt you, and you will have to confine yourself to the reasons, the real reasons for asking me to recuse myself.

MANDELA: Your Worship, the next point which I want to make is this: I raise the question, how can I be expected to believe that this same racial discrimination which has been the cause of so much injustice and suffering right through the years should now operate here to give me a fair and open trial? Is there no danger that an African accused may regard the courts not as impartial tribunals, dispensing justice without fear or favour, but as instruments used by the white man to punish those amongst us who clamour for deliverance from the fiery furnace of white rule. I have grave fears that this system of justice may enable the guilty to drag the innocent before the courts. It enables the unjust to prosecute and demand vengeance against the just. It may tend to lower the standards of fairness and justice applied in the country's courts by white judicial officers to black litigants. This is the first ground for this application: that I will not receive a fair and proper trial.

The second ground of my objection is that I consider myself neither morally nor legally obliged to obey laws made by a parliament in which I am not represented.

That the will of the people is the basis of the authority of government is a principle universally acknowledged as sacred throughout the civilised world, and constitutes the basic foundations of freedom and justice. It is understandable why citizens, who have the vote as well as the right to direct representation in the country's governing bodies, should be morally and legally bound by the laws governing the country.

It should be equally understandable why we, as Africans, should adopt the attitude that we are neither morally nor legally bound to obey laws which we have not made, nor can we be expected to have confidence in courts which enforce such laws.

I am aware that in many cases of this nature in the past, South African courts have upheld the right of the African people to work for democratic changes. Some of our judicial officers have even openly criticised the policy which refuses to acknowledge that all men are born free and equal, and fearlessly condemned the denial of opportunities to our people.

But such exceptions exist in spite of, not because of, the grotesque system of justice that has been built up in this country. These exceptions furnish yet another proof that even among the country's whites there are honest men whose sense of fairness and justice revolts against the cruelty perpetrated by their own white brothers to our people.

The existence of genuine democratic values among some of the country's whites in the judiciary, however slender they may be, is welcomed by me. But I have no illusions about the significance of this fact, healthy a sign as it might be. Such honest and upright whites are few and they have certainly not succeeded in convincing the vast majority of the rest of the white population that white supremacy leads to dangers and disaster.

However, it would be a hopeless commandant who relied for his victories on the few soldiers in the enemy camp who sympathise with his cause. A competent general pins his faith on the superior striking power he commands and on the justness of his cause which he must pursue uncompromisingly to the bitter end.

I hate race discrimination most intensely and in all its manifestations. I have fought it all during my life; I fight it now, and will do so until the end of my days. Even although I now happen to be tried by one whose opinion I hold in high esteem, I detest most violently the set-up that surrounds me here. It makes me feel that I am a black man in a white man's court. This should not be. I should feel perfectly at ease and at home with the assurance that I am being tried by a fellow South African who does not regard me as an inferior, entitled to a special type of justice.

This is not the type of atmosphere most conducive to feelings of security and confidence in the impartiality of a court.

The court might reply to this part of my argument by assuring me that it will try my case fairly and without fear or favour, that in deciding whether or not I am guilty of the offence charged by the State, the court will not be influenced by the colour of my skin or by any other improper motive.

That might well be so. But such a reply would completely miss the point of my argument.

As already indicated, my objection is not directed to Your Worship in his personal capacity, nor is it intended to reflect upon the integrity of the court. My objection is based upon the fact that our courts, as presently constituted, create grave doubts in the minds of an African accused, whether he will receive a fair and proper trial.

This doubt springs from objective facts relating to the practice of unfair discrimination against the black man in the constitution of the country's courts. Such doubts cannot be allayed by mere verbal assurances from a presiding officer, however sincere such assurances might be. There is only one way, and one way only, of allaying such doubts, namely, by removing unfair discrimination in judicial appointments. This is my first difficulty.

I have yet another difficulty about similar assurances Your Worship might give. Broadly speaking, Africans and whites in this country have no common standard of fairness, morality, and ethics, and it would be very difficult to determine on my part what standard of fairness and justice Your Worship has in mind.

In their relationship with us, South African whites regard it as fair and just to pursue policies which have outraged the conscience of mankind and of honest and upright men throughout the civilised world. They suppress our aspirations, bar our way to freedom, and deny us opportunities to promote our moral and material progress, to secure ourselves from fear and want. All the good things of life are reserved for the white folk and we blacks are expected to be content to nourish our bodies with such pieces of food as drop from the tables of men with white skins. This is the white man's standard of justice and fairness. Herein lies his conceptions of ethics. Whatever he himself may say in his defence, the white man's moral standards in this country must be judged by the extent to which he has condemned the vast majority of its inhabitants to serfdom and inferiority.

We, on the other hand, regard the struggle against colour discrimination and for the pursuit of freedom and happiness as the highest aspiration of all men. Through bitter experience, we have learnt to regard the white man as a harsh and merciless type of human being whose contempt for our rights, and whose utter indifference to the promotion of our welfare, makes his assurances to us absolutely meaningless and hypocritical.

I have the hope and confidence that Your Worship will not hear this objection lightly nor regard it as frivolous. I have decided to speak frankly and honestly because the injustice I have referred to contains the seeds of an extremely dangerous situation for our country and people. I make no threat when I say that unless these wrongs are remedied without delay, we might well find that even plain talk before the country's courts is too timid a method to draw the attention of the country to our political demands.

Finally, I need only to say that the courts have said that the possibility of bias and not actual bias is all that needs be proved to ground an application of this nature. In this application I have merely referred to certain objective facts, from which I submit that the possibility be inferred that I will not receive a fair and proper trial.

MAGISTRATE: Mr. Prosecutor, have you anything to say?

PROSECUTOR: Very briefly, Your Worship, I just wish to point out that there are certain legal grounds upon which an accused person is entitled to apply for the recusal of a judicial officer from the case in which he is to be tried. I submit that the Accused's application is not based on one of those principles, and I ask the Court to reject it.

MAGISTRATE: [to Mandela] Your application is dismissed. Will you now plead to your charges?

MANDELA: I plead *not guilty* to both charges, to all the charges.

(Editor's Note: One of the witnesses was the secretary to Prime Minister Verwoerd. Mandela questioned him about a letter that the ANC had sent to the Prime Minister.)

[reading the letter] "I am directed by the All-in African National Action Council to address your government in the following terms:

"The All-in African National Action Council was established in terms of a resolution adopted at a conference held at Pietermaritzburg on 25 and 26 March 1961. This conference was attended by 1,500 delegates from town and country, representing 145 religious, social, cultural, sporting, and political bodies.

"Conference noted that your government, after receiving a mandate from a section of the European population, decided to proclaim a republic on 31 May.

"It was the firm view of delegates that your government, which represents only a minority of the population in this country, is not entitled to take such a decision without first seeking the views and obtaining the express consent of the African people. Conference feared that under this proposed republic your government, which is already notorious the world over for its obnoxious policies, would continue to make even more savage attacks on the rights and living conditions of the African people.

"Conference carefully considered the grave political situation facing the African people today. Delegate after delegate drew attention to the vicious manner in which your government forced the people of Zeerust, Sekhukhuniland, Pondoland, Nongoma, Tembuland and other areas to accept the unpopular system of Bantu Authorities, and pointed to numerous facts and incidents which indicate the rapid manner in which race relations are deteriorating in this country.

"It was the earnest opinion of Conference that this dangerous situation could be averted only by the calling of a sovereign national convention representative of all South Africans, to draw up a new non-racial and democratic Constitution. Such a convention would discuss our national problems in a sane and sober manner, and would work out solutions which sought to preserve and safeguard the interests of all sections of the population.

"Conference unanimously decided to call upon your government to summon such a convention before 31 May.

"Conference further decided that unless your government calls the convention before the above-mentioned date, countrywide demonstrations would be held on the eve of the republic in protest. Conference also resolved that in addition to the demonstrations, the African people would be called upon to refuse to co-operate with the proposed republic.

"We attach the Resolutions of the Conference for your attention and necessary action.

"We now demand that your government call the convention before 31 May, failing which we propose to adopt the steps indicated in paragraphs 8 and 9 of this letter.

"These demonstrations will be conducted in a disciplined and peaceful manner.

"We are fully aware of the implications of this decision, and the action we propose taking. We have no illusions about the counter-measures your government might take in this matter. After all, South Africa and the world know that during the last thirteen years your government has subjected us to merciless and arbitrary rule. Hundreds of our people have been banned and confined to certain areas. Scores have been banished to remote parts of the country, and many arrested and jailed for a multitude of offences. It has become extremely difficult to hold meetings, and freedom of speech has been drastically curtailed. During the last twelve months we have gone through a period of grim dictatorship, during which seventy-five people were killed and hundreds injured while peacefully demonstrating against passes.

"Political organisations were declared unlawful, and thousands flung into jail without trial. Your government can only take these measures to suppress the forthcoming demonstrations, and these measures have failed to stop opposition to the policies of your government. We are not deterred by threats of force and violence made by you and your government, and will carry out our duty without flinching."

MANDELA: You remember the contents of this letter?

WITNESS: I do.

MANDELA: Did you place this letter before your Prime Minister?

WITNESS: Yes.

MANDELA: On what date? Can you remember?

WITNESS: It is difficult to remember, but I gather from the date specified on the date stamp, the Prime Minister's Office date stamp.

MANDELA: That is 24 April. Now was any reply given to this letter by the Prime Minister? Did he reply to this letter?

WITNESS: He did not reply to the writer.

MANDELA: He did not reply to the letter. Now, will you agree that this letter raises matters of vital concern to the vast majority of the citizens of this country?

WITNESS: I do not agree.

MANDELA: You don't agree? You don't agree that the question of human rights, of civil liberties, is a matter of vital importance to the African people?

WITNESS: Yes, that is so, indeed.

MANDELA: Are these things mentioned here?

WITNESS: Yes, I think so.

MANDELA: They are mentioned. You agree that this letter deals with matters of vital importance to the African people in this country? You have already agreed that this letter raises questions like the rights of freedom, civil liberties, and so on?

WITNESS: Yes, the letter raises it.

MANDELA: Important questions to any citizen?

WITNESS: Yes.

MANDELA: Now, you know of course that Africans don't enjoy the rights demanded in this letter. They are denied the rights of government?

WITNESS: Some rights.

MANDELA: No African is a member of parliament?

WITNESS: That is right.

MANDELA: No African can be a member of the Provincial Council, of the Municipal Councils?

WITNESS: Yes.

MANDELA: Africans have no vote in this country?

WITNESS: They have got no vote as far as parliament is concerned.

MANDELA: Yes, that is what I am talking about, I am talking about parliament, and other government bodies of the country, the Provincial Councils, the Municipal Councils. They have no vote?

WITNESS: That is right.

MANDELA: Would you agree with me that in any civilised country in the world it would be at least most scandalous for a Prime Minister to fail to reply to a letter raising vital issues affecting the majority of the citizens of that country. Would you agree with that?

WITNESS: I don't agree with that.

MANDELA: You don't agree that it would be irregular for a Prime Minister to ignore a letter raising vital issues affecting the vast majority of the citizens of that country?

WITNESS: This letter has not been ignored by the Prime Minister.

MANDELA: Just answer the question. Do you regard it proper for a Prime Minister not to respond to pleas made in regard to vital issues by the vast majority of the citizens of the country? You say that is not wrong?

WITNESS: The Prime Minister did respond to the letter.

MANDELA: Mr. Barnard, I don't want to be rude to you. Will you confine yourself to answering my questions? The question I am putting to you is, do you agree that it is most improper on the part of a Prime Minister not to reply to a communication raising vital issues affecting the vast majority of the country?

WITNESS: I do not agree in this special case, because . . .

MANDELA: As a general proposition? Would you regard it as improper, speaking generally, for a Prime Minister not to respond to a letter of this nature, that is, a letter raising vital issues affecting the majority of the citizens?

PROSECUTOR: (*Intervened with objections to the line of questioning*)

MANDELA: You say that the Prime Minister did not ignore this letter?

WITNESS: He did not acknowledge the letter to the writer.

MANDELA: This letter was not ignored by the Prime Minister?

WITNESS: No, it was not ignored.

MANDELA: It was attended to?

WITNESS: It was indeed.

MANDELA: In what way?

WITNESS: According to the usual procedure, and that is that the Prime Minister refers correspondence to the respective Minister, the Minister most responsible for that particular letter.

MANDELA: Was this letter referred to another Department?

WITNESS: That is right.

MANDELA: Which Department?

WITNESS: The Department of Justice.

MANDELA: Can you explain why I was not favoured with the courtesy of an acknowledgement of this letter, and also the explanation that it had been referred to the appropriate Department for attention?

WITNESS: When a letter is replied to and whether it should be replied to, depends on the contents of the letter in many instances.

MANDELA: My question is, can you explain to me why I was not favoured with the courtesy of an acknowledgement of the letter, irrespective of what the Prime Minister is going to do about it? Why was I not favoured with this courtesy?

WITNESS: Because of the contents of this letter.

MANDELA: Because it raises vital issues?

WITNESS: Because of the contents of the letter.

MANDELA: I see. This is not the type of thing the Prime Minister would ever consider responding to?

WITNESS: The Prime Minister did respond.

MANDELA: You say that the issues raised in this letter are not the type of thing your Prime Minister could ever respond to?

WITNESS: The whole tone of the letter was taken into consideration.

MANDELA: The tone of the letter demanding a National Convention? Of all South Africans? That is the tone of the letter? That is not the type of thing your Prime Minister could ever respond to?

WITNESS: The tone of the letter indicates whether, and to what extent, the Prime Minister responds to correspondence.

MANDELA: I want to put it to you that in failing to respond to this letter, your Prime Minister fell below the standards which one expects from one in such a position.

Now this letter, Exhibit 18, is dated 26 June 1961, and it is also addressed to the Prime Minister, and it reads as follows:

"I refer you to my letter of 20 April 1961, to which you do not have the courtesy to reply or acknowledge receipt. In the letter referred to above I informed you of the resolutions passed by the All-in African National Conference in Pietermaritzburg on 26 March 1961, demanding the calling by your government before 31 May 1961 of a multi-racial and sovereign National Convention to draw up a new non-racial and democratic Constitution for South Africa. The Conference Resolution which was attached to my letter indicated that if your government did not call this convention by the specific date, countrywide demonstrations would be staged to mark our protest against the White republic forcibly imposed on us by a minority. The Resolution further indicated that in addition to the demonstrations, the African people would be called upon not to co-operate with the republican government, or with any government based on force. As your government did not respond to our demands, the All-in African National Council, which was entrusted by the Conference with the task of implementing its resolutions, called for a General Strike on the 29, 30 and 31 of last month. As predicted in my letter of 30 April 1961, your government sought to suppress the strike by force. You rushed a special law in parliament authorising the detention without trial of people connected with the organisation of the strike. The army was mobilised and European civilians armed. More than ten thousand innocent Africans were arrested under the pass laws, and meetings banned throughout the country. Long before the factory gates were opened on Monday, 29 May 1961, senior police officers and Nationalist South Africans spread a deliberate falsehood and announced that the strike had failed. All these measures failed to break the strike and our people stood up magnificently and gave us solid and substantial support. Factory and office workers, businessmen in town and country, students in university colleges, in the primary and secondary schools, rose to the occasion and recorded in clear terms their opposition to the republic. The government is guilty of self-deception if they say that non-Europeans did not respond to the call.

Considerations of honesty demand of your government to realise that the African people who constitute four-fifths of the country's population are against your republic. As indicated above, the Pietermaritzburg resolution provided that in addition to the countrywide demonstrations, the African people would refuse to co-operate with the republic or any form of government based on force. Failure by your government to call the convention makes it imperative for us to launch a full-scale and countrywide campaign for non-co-operation with your government. There are two alternatives before you. Either you accede to our demands and call a National Convention of all South Africans to draw up a democratic Constitution, which will end the frightful policies of racial oppression pursued by your government. By pursuing this course and abandoning the repressive and dangerous policies of your government, you may still save our country from economic dislocation and ruin and from civil strife and bitterness. Alternatively, you may choose to persist with the present policies, which are cruel and dishonest and which are opposed by millions of people here and abroad. For our own part, we wish to make it perfectly clear that we shall never cease to fight against repression and injustice, and we are resuming active opposition against your regime. In taking this decision we must again stress that we have no illusions of the serious implications of our decision. We know that your government will once again unleash all its fury and barbarity to persecute the African people. But as the result of the last strike has clearly proved, no power on earth can stop an oppressed people determined to win their freedom. History punishes those who resort to force and fraud to suppress the claims and legitimate aspirations of the majority of the country's citizens."

MANDELA: This is the letter which you received on 28 June 1961? Again there was no acknowledgement or reply by the Prime Minister to this letter?

WITNESS: I don't think it is — I think it shouldn't be called a letter in the first instance, but an accumulation of threats.

MANDELA: Whatever it is, there was no reply to it?

WITNESS: No.

(Editor's Note: Mandela questioned an officer of the Special Branch of the police.)

MANDELA: Is it true to say that the present constitution of South Africa was passed at a National Convention representing whites only?

WITNESS: I don't know, I was not there.

MANDELA: But from your knowledge?

WITNESS: I don't know, I was not there.

MANDELA: You don't know at all?

WITNESS: No, I don't know.

MANDELA: You want this court to believe that, that you don't know?

WITNESS: I don't know, I was not there.

MANDELA: Just let me put the question. You don't know that the National Convention in 1909 was a convention of whites only?

WITNESS: I don't know, I was not there.

MANDELA: Do you know that the Union Parliament is an all-White parliament?

WITNESS: Yes, with representation for non-Whites.

MANDELA: Now, I just want to ask you one or two personal questions. What standard of education have you passed?

WITNESS: Matriculation.

MANDELA: When was that?

WITNESS: In 1932.

MANDELA: In what medium did you write it?

WITNESS: In my mother tongue. [Afrikaans]

MANDELA: I notice you are very proud of this?

WITNESS: I am.

MANDELA: You know of course that in this country we have no language rights as Africans?

WITNESS: I don't agree with you.

MANDELA: None of our languages is an official language, for example. Would you agree with that?

WITNESS: They are perhaps not in the Statute Book as official languages, but no one forbids you from using your own language.

MANDELA: Will you answer the question? Is it true that in this country there are only two official languages, and they are English and Afrikaans?

WITNESS: I agree entirely. By name they are the two official languages, but no one has ever forbidden you to use your own language.

MANDELA: Is it true that there are only two official languages in this country, that is English and Afrikaans?

WITNESS: To please you, that is so.

MANDELA: Is it true that the Afrikaner people in this country have fought for equality of English and Afrikaans? There was a time, for example, when Afrikaans was not the official language in the history of the various colonies, like the Cape?

WITNESS: Yes, I agree with you entirely. Constitutionally, the Afrikaner did fight for his language but not through agitators.

(Editor's Note; Duiring the trial, Mandela once again asked for a recusal.)

MANDELA: I want to make application for the recusal of Your Worship from this case. As I indicated last Monday, I hold

Your Worship in high esteem, and I do not for one single moment doubt Your Worship's sense of fairness and justice. I still do, as I assured Your Worship last Monday. I make this application with the greatest of respect. I have been placed in possession of information to the effect that after the adjournment yesterday, Your Worship was seen leaving the courtroom in the company of Warrant Officer Dirker of the Special Branch, and another member of the Special Branch. As Your Worship will remember, Warrant Officer Dirker gave evidence in this case on the first day of the trial. The State Prosecutor then indicated that he would be called later, on another aspect of this case. I was then given permission by the court to defer my cross examination of this witness until then. The second member of the Special Branch who was in the company of Your Worship, has been seen throughout this trial assisting the State Prosecutor in presenting the case against me. Your Worship was seen entering a small blue Volkswagen car; it is believed that Your Worship sat in front, as Warrant Officer Dirker drove the car. And this other member of the Special Branch sat behind. At about ten to two Your Worship was seen returning with Warrant Officer Dirker and this other member of the Special Branch.

Now, it is not known what communication passed between Your Worship and Warrant Officer Dirker and this other member of the Special Branch. I, as an accused, was not there, and was not represented. Now, these facts have created an impression in my mind that the court has associated itself with the State case. I am left with the substantial fear that justice is being administered in a secret manner. It is an elementary rule of justice that a judicial officer should not communicate or associate in any manner whatsoever with a party to those proceedings. I submit that Your Worship should not have acted in this fashion, and I must therefore ask Your Worship to recuse yourself from this case.

MAGISTRATE: I can only say this, that it is not for me here to give you any reasons. I can assure you, as I here now do, that

I did not communicate with these two gentlemen, and your application is refused.

(Editor's Note; Mandela questions an Indian officer in the Special Branch.)

MANDELA: You know about the Group Areas Act?

WITNESS: I do.

MANDELA: You know that it is intended to set certain areas for occupation by the various population groups in the country?

WITNESS: Yes, I do know.

MANDELA: And you know that it has aroused a great deal of feeling and opposition from the Indian community in this country?

WITNESS: Well, not that I know of. I think that most of the Indians are satisfied with it.

MANDELA: Is this a sincere opinion?

WITNESS: That is my sincere opinion, from people that I have met.

MANDELA: And are you aware of the attitude of the South African Indian Congress, about the Group Areas?

WITNESS: Yes.

MANDELA: What is the attitude of the South African Indian Congress?

WITNESS: The South African Indian Congress is against it.

MANDELA: And the attitude of the Transvaal Indian Congress?

WITNESS: Also.

MANDELA: They are against it?

WITNESS: Yes.

MANDELA: And the Transvaal Indian Youth Congress?

WITNESS: Also.

MANDELA: The Cape Indian Assembly, also against it?

WITNESS: Yes. Well, the Cape Indian Assembly I do not know about.

MANDELA: Well, you can take it from me that it is against it. Now, of course, if the Group Areas Act is carried out in its present form, it means that a large number of Indian merchants would lose their trading rights in areas which have been declared White Areas?

WITNESS: That is right.

MANDELA: And a large number of members of the Indian community who are living at the present moment in areas which might or have been declared as White Areas, would have to leave those homes, and have to go where they are to be stationed?

WITNESS: I think they will be better off than where . . .

MANDELA: Answer the question. You know that?

WITNESS: Yes, I know that.

MANDELA: You say that the Indian merchant class in this country, who are going to lose their business rights, are happy about it?

WITNESS: Well, not all.

MANDELA: Not all. And you are saying that those members of the Indian community who are going to be driven away from the areas where they are living at present would be happy to do so?

WITNESS: Yes, they would be.

MANDELA: Well, Mr. Moolla, I want to leave it at that, but just to say that you have lost your soul.

(Editor's Note; Mandela's address to the court)

I am charged with inciting people to commit an offence by way of protest against the law, a law which neither I nor any of my people had any say in preparing. The law against which the protest was directed is the law which established a republic in the Union of South Africa. I am also charged with leaving the country without a passport. This court has found that I am guilty of incitement to commit an offence in opposition to this law as well as of leaving the country. But in weighing up the decision as to the sentence which is to be imposed for such an offence, the court must take into account the question of responsibility, whether it is I who is responsible or whether, in fact, a large measure of the responsibility does not lie on the shoulders of the government which promulgated that law, knowing that my people, who constitute the majority of the population of this country, were opposed to that law, and knowing further that every legal means of demonstrating that opposition had been closed to them by prior legislation, and by government administrative action.

The starting point in the case against me is the holding of the conference in Pietermaritzburg on 25 and 26 March last year, known as the All-in African Conference, which was called by a committee which had been established by leading people and spokesmen of the whole African population, to consider the situation which was being created by the promulgation of the republic in the country, without consultation with us, and without our consent. That conference unanimously rejected the decision of the government, acting only in the name of and with the agreement of the white minority of this country, to establish a republic.

It is common knowledge that the conference decided that, in place of the unilateral proclamation of a republic by the white minority of South Africans only, it would demand in the name of the African people the calling of a truly national convention representative of all South Africans, irrespective of their colour, black and white, to sit amicably round a table, to debate a new constitution for South Africa, which was in essence what the government was doing by the proclamation of a republic, and furthermore, to press on behalf of the African people, that such new constitution should differ from the constitution of the proposed South African Republic by guaranteeing democratic rights on a basis of full equality to all South Africans of adult age. The conference had assembled, knowing full well that for a long period the present National Party Government of the Union of South Africa had refused to deal with, to discuss with, or to take into consideration the views of, the overwhelming majority of the South African population on this question. And, therefore, it was not enough for this conference just to proclaim its aim, but it was also necessary for the conference to find a means of stating that aim strongly and powerfully, despite the government's unwillingness to listen.

Accordingly, it was decided that should the government fail to summon such a National Convention before 31 May 1961, all sections of the population would be called on to stage a general strike for a period of three days, both to mark our protest against the establishment of a republic, based completely on white domination over a non-white majority, and also, in a last attempt to persuade the government to heed our legitimate claims, and thus to avoid a period of increasing bitterness and hostility and discord in South Africa.

At that conference, an Action Council was elected, and I became its secretary. It was my duty, as secretary of the committee, to establish the machinery necessary for publicising the decision of this conference and for directing the campaign of propaganda, publicity, and organisation which would flow from it.

The court is aware of the fact that I am an attorney by profession and no doubt the question will be asked why I, as an attorney who is bound, as part of my code of behaviour, to observe the laws of the country and to respect its customs and traditions, should willingly lend myself to a campaign whose ultimate aim was to bring about a strike against the proclaimed policy of the government of this country.

In order that the court shall understand the frame of mind which leads me to action such as this, it is necessary for me to explain the background to my own political development and to try to make this court aware of the factors which influenced me in deciding to act as I did.

Many years ago, when I was a boy brought up in my village in the Transkei, I listened to the elders of the tribe telling stories about the good old days, before the arrival of the white man. Then our people lived peacefully, under the democratic rule of their kings and their *amapakati*, and moved freely and confidently up and down the country without let or hindrance. Then the country was ours, in our own name and right. We occupied the land, the forests, the rivers; we extracted the mineral wealth beneath the soil and all the riches of this beautiful country. We set up and operated our own government, we controlled our own armies and we organised our own trade and commerce. The elders would tell tales of the wars fought by our ancestors in defence of the fatherland, as well as the acts of valour performed by generals and soldiers during those epic days. The names of Dingane and Bambata, among the Zulus, of Hintsa, Makana, Ndlambe of the AmaXhosa, of Sekhukhuni and others in the north, were mentioned as the pride and glory of the entire African nation.

I hoped and vowed then that, among the treasures that life might offer me, would be the opportunity to serve my people and make my own humble contribution to their freedom struggles.

The structure and organisation of early African societies in this country fascinated me very much and greatly influenced the evolution of my political outlook. The land, then the main means of production, belonged to the whole tribe, and there was no individual ownership whatsoever. There were no classes, no rich or poor and no exploitation of man by man. All men were free and equal and this was the foundation of government. Recognition of this general principle found expression in the constitution of the council, variously called

Imbizo, or Pitso, or Kgotla, which governs the affairs of the tribe. The council was so completely democratic that all members of the tribe could participate in its deliberations. Chief and subject, warrior and medicine man, all took part and endeavoured to influence its decisions. It was so weighty and influential a body that no step of any importance could ever be taken by the tribe without reference to it.

There was much in such a society that was primitive and insecure and it certainly could never measure up to the demands of the present epoch. But in such a society are contained the seeds of revolutionary democracy in which none will be held in slavery or servitude, and in which poverty, want, and insecurity shall be no more. This is the inspiration which, even today, inspires me and my colleagues in our political struggle.

When I reached adult stature, I became a member of the African National Congress. That was in 1944 and I have followed its policy, supported it, and believed in its aims and outlook for eighteen years. Its policy was one which appealed to my deepest inner convictions. It sought for the unity of all Africans, overriding tribal differences among them. It sought the acquisition of political power for Africans in the land of their birth. The African National Congress further believed that all people, irrespective of the national groups to which they may belong, and irrespective of the colour of their skins, all people whose home is South Africa and who believe in the principles of democracy and of equality of men, should be treated as Africans; that all South Africans are entitled to live a free life on the basis of fullest equality of the rights and opportunities in every field, of full democratic rights, with a direct say in the affairs of the government.

These principles have been embodied in the Freedom Charter, which none in this country will dare challenge for its place as the most democratic programme of political principles ever enunciated by any political party or organisation in this country. It was for me a matter of joy and pride to be a member of an organisation which has proclaimed so democratic a policy and which campaigned for it militantly and fearlessly. The principles enumerated in the Charter have not been those of African people alone, for whom the African National Congress has always been the spokesman. Those principles have been adopted as well by the Indian people and the South African Indian Congress; by a section of the Coloured people, through the South African Coloured People's Congress, and also by a farsighted, forward-looking section of the European population, whose organisation in days gone by was the South African Congress of Democrats. All these organisations, like the African National Congress, supported completely the demand for one man, one vote.

Right at the beginning of my career as an attorney I encountered difficulties imposed on me because of the colour of my skin, and further difficulty surrounding me because of my membership and support of the African National Congress. I discovered, for example, that, unlike a white attorney, I could not occupy business premises in the city unless I first obtained ministerial consent in terms of the Urban Areas Act. I applied for that consent, but it was never granted. Although I subsequently obtained a permit, for a limited period, in terms of the Group Areas Act, that soon expired, and the authorities refused to renew it. They insisted that my partner, Oliver Tambo, and I should leave the city and practise in an African location at the back of beyond, miles away from where clients could reach us during working hours. This was tantamount to asking us to abandon our legal practice, to give up the legal service of our people, for which we had spent many years training. No attorney worth his salt will agree easily to do so. For some years, therefore, we continued to occupy premises in the city, illegally. The threat of prosecution and ejection hung menacingly over us throughout that period. It was an act of defiance of the law. We were aware that it was, but, nevertheless, that act had been forced on us against our wishes, and we could do no other than to choose between compliance with the law and compliance with our consciences.

In the courts where we practised we were treated courteously by many officials but we were very often discriminated against by some and treated with resentment and hostility by others. We were constantly aware that no matter how well, how correctly, how adequately we pursued our career of law, we could not become a prosecutor, or a magistrate, or a judge. We became aware of the fact that as attorneys we often dealt with officials whose competence and attainments were no higher than ours, but whose superior position was maintained and protected by a white skin.

I regarded it as a duty which I owed, not just to my people, but also to my profession, to the practice of law, and to justice for all mankind, to cry out against this discrimination, which is essentially unjust and opposed to the whole basis of the attitude towards justice which is part of the tradition of legal training in this country. I believed that in taking up a stand against this injustice I was upholding the dignity of what should be an honourable profession.

Nine years ago the Transvaal Law Society applied to the Supreme Court to have my name struck off the roll because of the part I had played in a campaign initiated by the African National Congress, a campaign for the Defiance of Unjust Laws. During the campaign more than eight thousand of the most advanced and farseeing of my people deliberately courted arrest and imprisonment by breaking specified laws, which we regarded then, as we still do now, as unjust and repressive. In the opinion of the Law Society, my activity in connection with that campaign did not conform to the standards of conduct expected from members of our honourable profession, but on this occasion the Supreme Court held that I had been within my rights as an attorney, that there was nothing dishonourable in an attorney identifying himself with his people in their struggle for political rights, even if his activities should infringe upon the laws of the country; the Supreme Court rejected the application of the Law Society.

It would not be expected that with such a verdict in my favour I should discontinue my political activities. But Your Worship may well wonder why it is that I should find it necessary to persist with such conduct, which has not only brought me the difficulties I have referred to, but which has resulted in my spending some four years on a charge before the courts of high treason, of which I was subsequently acquitted, and of many months in jail on no charge at all, merely on the basis of the government's dislike of my views and of my activities during the whole period of the Emergency of 1960.

Your Worship, I would say that the whole life of any thinking African in this country drives him continuously to a conflict between his conscience on the one hand and the law on the other. This is not a conflict peculiar to this country. The conflict arises for men of conscience, for men who think and who feel deeply in every country. Recently in Britain, a peer of the realm, Earl Russell, probably the most respected philosopher of the Western world, was sentenced, convicted for precisely the type of activities for which I stand before you today, for following his conscience in defiance of the law, as a protest against a nuclear weapons policy being followed by his own government. For him, his duty to the public, his belief in the morality of the essential rightness of the cause for which he stood, rose superior to this high respect for the law. He could not do other than to oppose the law and to suffer the consequences for it. Nor can I. Nor can many Africans in this country. The law as it is applied, the law as it has been developed over a long period of history, and especially the law as it is written and designed by the Nationalist government, is a law which, in our view, is immoral, unjust, and intolerable. Our consciences dictate that we must protest against it, that we must oppose it, and that we must attempt to alter it.

Always we have been conscious of our obligations as citizens to avoid breaches of the law, where such breaches can be avoided, to prevent a clash between the authorities and our people, where such clash can be prevented, but nevertheless, we have been driven to speak up for what we believe is right, and to work for it and to try and bring about changes which will satisfy our human conscience.

Throughout its fifty years of existence the African National Congress, for instance, has done everything possible to bring its demands to the attention of successive South African governments. It has sought at all times peaceful solutions for all the country's ills and problems. The history of the ANC is filled with instances where deputations were sent to South African governments either on specific issues or on the general political demands of our people. I do not wish to burden Your Worship by enunciating the occasions when such deputations were sent; all that I wish to indicate at this stage is that, in addition to the efforts made by former presidents of the ANC, when Mr. Strijdom became Prime Minister of this country, my leader, Chief A J Lutuli, then President of our organisation, made yet another effort to persuade this government to consider and to heed our point of view. In his letter to the Prime Minister at the time, Chief Lutuli exhaustively reviewed the country's relations and its dangers, and expressed the view that a meeting between the government and African leaders had become necessary and urgent.

This statesmanlike and correct behaviour on the part of the leader of the majority of the South African population did not find an appropriate answer from the leader of the South African government. The standard of behaviour of the South African government towards my people and its aspirations has not always been what it should have been, and is not always the standard which is to be expected in serious high-level dealings between civilised peoples. Chief Lutuli's letter was not even favoured with the courtesy of an acknowledgement from the Prime Minister's office.

This experience was repeated after the Pietermaritzburg conference, when I, as Secretary of the Action Council, elected at that conference, addressed a letter to the Prime Minister, Dr Verwoerd, informing him of the resolution which had been taken, and calling on him to initiate steps for the convening of such a national convention as we suggested, before the date specified in the resolution. In a civilised country one would be outraged by the failure of the head of government even to acknowledge receipt of a letter, or to consider such a reasonable request put to him by a broadly representative collection of important personalities and leaders of the most important community of the country. Once again, government standards in dealing with my people fell below what the civilised world would expect. No reply, no response whatsoever, was received to our letter, no indication was even given that it had received any consideration whatsoever. Here we, the African people, and especially we of the National Action Council, who had been entrusted with the tremendous responsibility of safeguarding the interests of the African people, were faced with this conflict between the law and our conscience. In the face of the complete failure of the government to heed, to consider, or even to respond to our seriously proposed objections and our solutions to the forthcoming republic, what were we to do? Were we to allow the law which states that you shall not commit an offence by way of protest, to take its course and thus betray our conscience and our belief? Were we to uphold our conscience and our beliefs to strive for what we believe is right, not just for us, but for all the people who live in this country, both the present generation and for generations to come, and thus transgress against the law? This is the dilemma which faced us, and in such a dilemma, men of honesty, men of purpose, and men of public morality and of conscience can only have one answer. They must follow the dictates of their conscience irrespective of the consequences which might overtake them for it. We of the Action Council, and I particularly as Secretary, followed my conscience.

If I had my time over I would do the same again, so would any man who dares call himself a man. We went ahead with our campaign as instructed by the conference and in accordance with its decisions.

The issue that sharply divided white South Africans during the referendum for a republic did not interest us. It formed no part in our campaign. Continued association with the British monarchy on the one hand, or the establishment of a Boer republic on the other — this was the crucial issue in so far as the White population was concerned and as it was put to them in the referendum. We are neither monarchists nor admirers of a *Voortrekker* type of republic. We believe that we were inspired by aspirations more worthy than either of the groups who took part in the campaign on these. We were inspired by the idea of bringing into being a democratic republic where all South Africans will enjoy human rights without the slightest discrimination; where African and non-African would be able to live together in peace, sharing a common nationality and a common loyalty to this country, which is our homeland. For these reasons we were opposed to the type of republic proposed by the Nationalist Party government, just as we have been opposed previously to the constitutional basis of the Union of South Africa as a part of the British Empire. We were not prepared to accept, at a time when constitutional changes were being made, that these constitutional changes should not affect the real basis of a South African constitution, white supremacy and white domination, the very basis which has brought South Africa and its constitution into contempt and disrepute throughout the world.

I wish now to deal with the campaign itself, with the character of the campaign, and with the course of events which followed our decision. From the beginning our campaign was a campaign designed to call on people as a last extreme, if all else failed, if all discussions failed to materialise, if the government showed no sign of taking any steps to attempt either to treat with us or to meet our demands peacefully, to strike, that is to stay away from work, and so to bring economic pressure to bear. There was never any intention that our demonstrations, at that stage, go further than that. In all our statements, both those which are before the court, and those which are not before the court, we made it clear that that strike would be a peaceful protest, in which people were asked to remain in their homes. It was our intention that the demonstration should go through peacefully and peaceably, without clash and conflict, as such demonstrations do in every civilised country.

Nevertheless, around that campaign and our preparations for that campaign was created the atmosphere for civil war and revolution. I would say deliberately created. Deliberately created not by us, Your Worship, but by the government, which set out from the beginning of this campaign not to treat with us, not to heed us, not to talk to us, but rather to present us as wild, dangerous revolutionaries, intent on disorder and riot, incapable of being dealt with in any way save by mustering an overwhelming force against us and the implementation of every possible forcible means, legal and illegal, to suppress us. The government behaved in a way no civilised government should dare behave when faced with a peaceful, disciplined, sensible, and democratic expression of the views of its own population. It ordered the mobilisation of its armed forces to attempt to cowe and terrorise our peaceful protest. It arrested people known to be active in African politics and in support of African demands for democratic rights, passed special laws enabling it to hold them without trial for twelve days instead of the forty eight hours which had been customary before, and hold them, the majority of them, never to be charged before the courts, but to be released after the date for the strike had passed. If there was a danger during this period that violence would result from the situation in the country, then the possibility was of the government's making. They set the scene for violence by relying exclusively on violence with which to answer our people and their demands. The countermeasures which they took clearly reflected growing uneasiness on their part, which grew out of the knowledge that their policy did not enjoy the support of the majority of the people, while ours did. It was clear that the government was attempting to combat the intensity of our campaign by a reign of terror. At the time the newspapers suggested the strike was a failure and it was said that we did not enjoy the support of the people. I deny that. I deny it and I will continue to deny it as long as this government is not prepared to put to the test the question of the opinion of the African people by consulting them in a democratic way. In any event, the evidence in this case has shown that it was a substantial success. Our campaign was an intensive campaign and met with tremendous and overwhelming response from the population. In the end, if a strike did not materialise on the scale on which it had been hoped it would, it was not because the people were not willing, but because the overwhelming strength, violence, and force of the government's attack against our campaign had for the time being achieved its aim of forcing us into submission against our wishes and against our conscience.

I wish again to return to the question of why people like me, knowing all this, knowing in advance that this government is incapable of progressive democratic moves so far as our people are concerned, knowing that this government is incapable of reacting towards us in any way other than by the use of overwhelming brute force, why I and people like me nevertheless decide to go ahead to do what we must do. We have been conditioned to our attitudes by the history which is not of our making. We have been conditioned by the history of White governments in this country to accept the fact that Africans, when they make their demands strongly and powerfully enough to have some chance of success, will be met by force and terror on the part of the government. This is not something we have taught the African people, this is something the African people have learned from their own bitter experience. We learned it from each successive government. We learned it from the government of General Smuts at the time of two massacres of our people: the 1921 massacre in Bulhoek when more than a hundred men, women, and children were killed, and from the 1924 massacre — the Bondelswart massacre in South-West Africa, in which some two hundred Africans were killed. We have continued to learn it from every successive government.

Government violence can do only one thing, and that is to breed counter violence. We have warned repeatedly that the government, by resorting continually to violence, will breed in this country counter-violence amongst the people, till ultimately, if there is no dawning of sanity on the part of the government — ultimately, the dispute between the government and my people will finish up by being settled in violence and by force. Already there are indications in this country that people, my people, Africans, are turning to deliberate acts of violence and of force against the government, in order to persuade the government, in the only language which this government shows by its own behaviour that it understands.

Elsewhere in the world, a court would say to me, "You should have made representations to the government." This court, I am confident, will not say so. Representations have been made, by people who have gone before me, time and time again. Representations were made in this case by me; I do not want again to repeat the experience of those representations. The court cannot expect a respect for the processes of representation and negotiation to grow amongst the African people, when the government shows every day, by its conduct, that it despises such processes and frowns upon them and will not indulge in them. Nor will the court, I believe, say that, under the circumstances, my people are condemned forever to say nothing and to do nothing. If this court says that, or believes it, I think it is mistaken and deceiving itself. Men are not capable of doing nothing, of saying nothing, of not reacting to injustice, of not protesting against oppression, of not striving for the good of society and the good life in the ways they see it. Nor will they do so in this country.

Perhaps the court will say that despite our human rights to protest, to object, to make ourselves heard, we should stay within the letter of the law. I would say, Sir, that it is the government, its administration of the law, which brings the law into such contempt and disrepute that one is no longer concerned in this country to stay within the letter of the law. I will illustrate this from my own experience. The government has used the process of law to handicap me, in my personal life, in my career, and in my political work, in a way which is calculated, in my opinion, to bring about a contempt for the law. In December 1952 I was issued with an order by the government, not as a result of a trial before a court and a conviction, but as a result of prejudice, or perhaps Star Chamber procedure behind closed doors in the halls of government. In terms of that order I was confined to the magisterial district of Johannesburg for six months and, at the same time, I was prohibited from attending gatherings for a similar period. That order expired in June 1953 and three months thereafter, again without any hearing, without any attempt to hear my side of the case, without facing me with charges, or explanations, both bans were renewed for a further period of two years. To these bans a third was added: I was ordered by the Minister of Justice to resign altogether from the African National Congress, and never again to become a member or to participate in its activities. Towards the end of 1955, I found myself free and able to move around once again, but not for long. In February 1956 the bans were again renewed, administratively, again without hearing, this time for five years. Again, by order of the government, in the name of the law, I found myself restricted and isolated from my fellow men, from people who think like me and believe like me. I found myself trailed by officers of the Security Branch of the Police Force wherever I went. In short, I found myself treated as a criminal—an unconvicted criminal. I was not allowed to pick my company, to frequent the company of men, to participate in their political activities, to join their organisations. I was not free from constant police surveillance. I was made, by the law, a criminal, not because of what I had done, but because of what I stood for, because of what I thought, because of my conscience. Can it be any wonder to anybody that such conditions make a man an outlaw of society? Can it be wondered that such a man, having been outlawed by the government, should be prepared to lead the life of an outlaw, as I have led for some months, according to the evidence before this court?

It has not been easy for me during the past period to separate myself from my wife and children, to say goodbye to the good old days when, at the end of a strenuous day at an office, I could look forward to joining my family at the dinner-table, and instead to take up the life of a man hunted continuously by the police, living separated from those who are closest to me, in my own country, facing continually the hazards of detection and of arrest. This has been a life infinitely more difficult than serving a prison sentence. No man in his right senses would voluntarily choose such a life in preference to the one of normal family social life which exists in every civilised community.

But there comes a time, as it came in my life, when a man is denied the right to live a normal life, when he can only live the life of an outlaw because the government has so decreed to use the law to impose a state of outlawry upon him. I was driven to this situation, and I do not regret having taken the decisions that I did take. Other people will be driven in the same way in this country, by this very same force of police persecution and of administrative action by the government, to follow my course, of that I am certain. The decision that I should continue to carry out the decisions of the Pietermaritzburg conference, despite police persecution all the time, was not my decision alone. It was a decision reached by me, in consultation with those who were entrusted with the leadership of the campaign and its fulfillment. It was clear to us then, in the early periods of the campaign, when the government was busy whipping up an atmosphere of hysteria as the prelude to violence, that the views of the African people would not be heard, would not find expression, unless attempts were made deliberately by those of us entrusted with the task of carrying through the strike call to keep away from the illegal, unlawful attacks of the Special Branch, the unlawful detention of people for twelve days without trial, and unlawful and illegal intervention by the police and the government forces in legitimate political activity of the population. I was, at the time of the Pietermaritzburg conference, free from bans for a short time, and a time which I had no reason to expect would prolong itself for very long. Had I remained in my normal surroundings, carrying on my normal life, I would have again been forced by government action to a position of an outlaw. That I was not prepared to do while the commands of the Pietermaritzburg conference to me remained unfulfilled. New situations require new tactics. The situation, which was not of our making, which followed the Pietermaritzburg conference required the tactics which I adopted, I believe, correctly.

A lot has been written since the Pietermaritzburg conference, and even more since my arrest, much of which is flattering to my pride and dear to my heart, but much of which is mistaken and incorrect. It has been suggested that the advances, the articulateness of our people, the successes which they are achieving here, and the recognition which they are winning both here and abroad are in some way the result of my work. I must place on record my belief that I have been only one in a large army of people, to all of whom the credit for any success of achievement is due. Advance and progress is not the result of my work alone, but of the collective work of my colleagues and I, both here and abroad. I have been fortunate throughout my political life to work together with colleagues whose abilities and contributions to the cause of my people's freedom have been greater and better than my own, people who have been loved and respected by the African population generally as a result of the dedicated way in which they have fought for freedom and for peace and justice in this country. It distresses me to read reports that my arrest has been instigated by some of my colleagues for some sinister purposes of their own. Nothing could be further from the truth. I dismiss these suggestions as the sensational inventions of unscrupulous journalists. People who stoop to such unscrupulous manoeuvres as the betrayal of their own comrades have no place in the good fight which I have fought for the freedom of the African people, which my colleagues continue to fight without me today. Not just I alone, but all of us are willing to pay the penalties which we may have to pay, which I may have to pay for having followed my conscience in pursuit of what I believe is right. So are we all. Many people in this country have paid the price before me, and many will pay the price after me.

I do not believe, Your Worship, that this court, in inflicting penalties on me for the crimes for which I am convicted, should be moved by the belief that penalties deter men from the course that they believe is right. History shows that penalties do not deter men when their conscience is aroused, nor will they deter my people or the colleagues with whom I have worked before.

I am prepared to pay the penalty even though I know how bitter and desperate is the situation of an African in the prisons of this country. I have been in these prisons and I know how gross is the discrimination, even behind the prison walls, against Africans, how much worse is the treatment meted out to African prisoners than that accorded to whites. Nevertheless, these considerations do not sway me from the path that I have taken, nor will they sway others like me. For to men, freedom in their own land is the pinnacle of their ambitions, from which nothing can turn men of conviction aside. More powerful than my fear of the dreadful conditions to which I might be subjected is my hatred for the dreadful conditions to which my people are subjected outside prison throughout this country.

I hate the practice of race discrimination, and in my hatred I am sustained by the fact that the overwhelming majority of mankind hate it equally. I hate the systematic inculcation of children with colour prejudice and I am sustained in that hatred by the fact that the overwhelming majority of mankind, here and abroad, are with me in that. I hate the racial arrogance which decrees that the good things of life shall be retained as the exclusive right of a minority of the population, and which reduces the majority of the population to a position of subservience and inferiority, and maintains them as voteless chattels to work where they are told and behave as they are told by the ruling minority. I am sustained in that hatred by the fact that the overwhelming majority of mankind both in this country and abroad are with me.

Nothing that this court can do to me will change in any way that hatred in me, which can only be removed by the removal of the injustice and the inhumanity which I have sought to remove from the political and social life of this country.

Whatever sentence Your Worship sees fit to impose upon me for the crime for which I have been convicted before this court, may it rest assured that when my sentence has been completed I will still be moved, as men are always moved, by their consciences; I will still be moved by my dislike of the race discrimination against my people when I come out from serving my sentence, to take up again, as best I can, the struggle for the removal of those injustices until they are finally abolished once and for all.

I now wish to deal with the Second Count.

When my colleagues and I received the invitation to attend the Conference of the Pan-African Freedom Movement for East and Central Africa, it was decided that I should leave the country and join our delegation to Addis Ababa, the capital of Ethiopia, where the conference would be held. It was part of my mandate to tour Africa and make direct contact with African leaders on the continent.

I did not apply for a passport because I knew very well that it would not be granted to me. After all, the Nationalist Party government, throughout the fourteen years of its oppressive rule, had refused permission to leave the country to many African scholars, educationalists, artists, sportsmen, and clerics, and I wished to waste none of my time by applying for a passport.

The tour of the continent made a forceful impression on me. For the first time in my life I was a free man; free from white oppression, from the idiocy of apartheid and racial arrogance, from police molestation, from humiliation and indignity.

Wherever I went I was treated like a human being. I met Rashidi Kawawa, Prime Minister of Tanganyika, and Julius Nyerere. I was received by Emperor Haile Selassie, by General Abboud, President of Sudan, by Habib Bourguiba, President of Tunisia, and by Modibo Keita of the Republic of Mali. I met Leopold Senghor, President of Senegal, Presidents Sekou Toure and Tubman, of Guinea and Liberia, respectively.

I met Ben Bella, the President of Algeria, and Colonel Boumedienne, the Commander-in-Chief of the Algerian Army of National Liberation. I saw the cream and flower of the Algerian youth who had fought French imperialism and whose valour had brought freedom and happiness to their country.

In London I was received by Hugh Gaitskell, Leader of the Labour Party, and by Jo Grimond, Leader of the Liberal Party, and other prominent Englishmen. I met Prime Minister Obote of Uganda, distinguished African nationalists like Kenneth Kaunda, Oginga Odinga, Joshua Nkomo, and many others. In all these countries we were showered with hospitality, and assured of solid support for our cause.

In its efforts to keep the African people in a position of perpetual subordination, South Africa must and will fail. South Africa is out of step with the rest of the civilised world, as is shown by the resolution adopted last night by the General Assembly of the United Nations Organisation which decided to impose diplomatic and economic sanctions. In the African states, I saw black and white mingling peacefully and happily in hotels, cinemas, trading in the same areas, using the same public transport, and living in the same residential areas.

I had to return home to report to my colleagues and to share my impressions and experiences with them.

I have done my duty to my people and to South Africa. I have no doubt that posterity will pronounce that I was innocent and that the criminals that should have been brought before this court are the members of the Verwoerd government.

"I am Prepared to Die"

Statement at the Rivonia Trial

April 20, 1964

I am the First Accused.

I hold a Bachelor's Degree in Arts and practised as an attorney in Johannesburg for a number of years in partnership with Oliver Tambo. I am a convicted prisoner serving five years for leaving the country without a permit and for inciting people to go on strike at the end of May 1961.

At the outset, I want to say that the suggestion made by the State in its opening that the struggle in South Africa is under the influence of foreigners or communists is wholly incorrect. I have done whatever I did, both as an individual and as a leader of my people, because of my experience in South Africa and my own proudly felt African background, and not because of what any outsider might have said.

In my youth in the Transkei I listened to the elders of my tribe telling stories of the old days. Amongst the tales they related to me were those of wars fought by our ancestors in defence of the fatherland. The names of Dingane and Bambata, Hintsa and Makana, Squngthi and Dalasile, Moshoeshoe and Sekhukhuni, were praised as the glory of the entire African nation. I hoped then that life might offer me the opportunity to serve my people and make my own humble contribution to their freedom struggle. This is what has motivated me in all that I have done in relation to the charges made against me in this case.

Having said this, I must deal immediately and at some length with the question of violence. Some of the things so far told to the Court are true and some are untrue. I do not, however, deny that I planned sabotage. I did not plan it in a spirit of recklessness, nor because I have any love of violence. I planned it as a result of a calm and sober assessment of the political situation that had arisen after many years of tyranny, exploitation, and oppression of my people by the Whites.

I admit immediately that I was one of the persons who helped to form Umkhonto we Sizwe, and that I played a prominent role in its affairs until I was arrested in August 1962.

In the statement which I am about to make I shall correct certain false impressions which have been created by State witnesses. Amongst other things, I will demonstrate that certain of the acts referred to in the evidence were not and could not have been committed by Umkhonto. I will also deal with the relationship between the African National Congress and Umkhonto, and with the part which I personally have played in the affairs of both organizations. I shall deal also with the part played by the Communist Party. In order to explain these matters properly, I will have to explain what Umkhonto set out to achieve; what methods it prescribed for the achievement of these objects, and why these methods were chosen. I will also have to explain how I became involved in the activities of these organizations.

I deny that Umkhonto was responsible for a number of acts which clearly fell outside the policy of the organisation, and which have been charged in the indictment against us. I do not know what justification there was for these acts, but to demonstrate that they could not have been authorized by Umkhonto, I want to refer briefly to the roots and policy of the organization.

I have already mentioned that I was one of the persons who helped to form Umkhonto. I, and the others who started the organization, did so for two reasons. Firstly, we believed that as a result of Government policy, violence by the African people had become inevitable, and that unless responsible leadership was given to canalize and control the feelings of our people, there would be outbreaks of terrorism which would produce an intensity of bitterness and hostility between the various races of this country which is not produced even by war. Secondly, we felt that without violence there would be no way open to the African people to succeed in their struggle against the principle of white supremacy. All lawful modes of expressing opposition to this principle had been closed by legislation, and we were placed in a position in which we had either to accept a permanent state of inferiority, or to defy the Government. We chose to defy the law. We first broke the law in a way which avoided any recourse to violence; when this form was legislated against, and then the Government resorted to a show of force to crush opposition to its policies, only then did we decide to answer violence with violence.

But the violence which we chose to adopt was not terrorism. We who formed Umkhonto were all members of the African National Congress, and had behind us the ANC tradition of non-violence and negotiation as a means of solving political disputes. We believe that South Africa belongs to all the people who live in it, and not to one group, be it black or white. We did not want an interracial war, and tried to avoid it to the last minute. If the Court is in doubt about this, it will be seen that the whole history of our organization bears out what I have said, and what I will subsequently say, when I describe the tactics which Umkhonto decided to adopt. I want, therefore, to say something about the African National Congress.

The African National Congress was formed in 1912 to defend the rights of the African people which had been seriously curtailed by the South Africa Act, and which were then being threatened by the Native Land Act. For thirty-seven years—that is until 1949—it adhered strictly to a constitutional struggle. It put forward demands and resolutions; it sent delegations to the Government in the belief that African grievances could be settled through peaceful discussion and that Africans could advance gradually to full political rights. But White Governments remained unmoved, and the rights of Africans became less instead of becoming greater. In the words of my leader, Chief Lutuli, who became President of the ANC in 1952, and who was later awarded the Nobel Peace Prize:

"Who will deny that thirty years of my life have been spent knocking in vain, patiently, moderately, and modestly at a closed and barred door? What have been the fruits of moderation? The past thirty years have seen the greatest number of laws restricting our rights and progress, until today we have reached a stage where we have almost no rights at all".

Even after 1949, the ANC remained determined to avoid violence. At this time, however, there was a change from the strictly constitutional means of protest which had been employed in the past. The change was embodied in a decision which was taken to protest against apartheid legislation by peaceful, but unlawful, demonstrations against certain laws. Pursuant to this policy the ANC launched the Defiance Campaign, in which I was placed in charge of volunteers. This campaign was based on the principles of passive resistance. More than 8,500 people defied apartheid laws and went to jail. Yet there was not a single instance of violence in the course of this campaign on the part of any defier. I and nineteen colleagues were convicted for the role which we played in organizing the campaign, but our sentences were suspended mainly because the Judge found that discipline and non-violence had been stressed throughout. This was the time when the volunteer section of the ANC was established, and when the word "Amadelakufa" was first used: this was the time when the volunteers were asked to take a pledge to uphold certain principles. Evidence dealing with volunteers and their pledges has been introduced into this case, but completely out of context. The volunteers were not, and are not, the soldiers of a black army pledged to fight a civil war against the whites. They were, and are, dedicated workers who are prepared to lead campaigns initiated by the ANC to distribute leaflets, to organize strikes, or do whatever the particular campaign required. They are called volunteers because they volunteer to face the penalties of imprisonment and whipping which are now prescribed by the legislature for such acts.

During the Defiance Campaign, the Public Safety Act and the Criminal Law Amendment Act were passed. These Statutes provided harsher penalties for offences committed by way of protests against laws. Despite this, the protests continued and the ANC adhered to its policy of non-violence. In 1956, 156 leading members of the Congress Alliance, including myself, were arrested on a charge of high treason and charges under the Suppression of Communism Act. The non-violent policy of the ANC was put in issue by the State, but when the Court gave judgment some five years later, it found that the ANC did not have a policy of violence. We were acquitted on all counts, which included a count that the ANC sought to set up a communist state in place of the existing regime. The Government has always sought to label all its opponents as communists. This allegation has been repeated in the present case, but as I will show, the ANC is not, and never has been, a communist organization.

In 1960 there was the shooting at Sharpeville, which resulted in the proclamation of a state of emergency and the declaration of the ANC as an unlawful organization. My colleagues and I, after careful consideration, decided that we would not obey this decree. The African people were not part of the Government and did not make the laws by which they were governed. We believed in the words of the Universal Declaration of Human Rights, that "the will of the people shall be the basis of authority of the Government", and for us to accept the banning was equivalent to accepting the silencing of the Africans for all time. The ANC refused to dissolve, but instead went underground. We believed it was our duty to preserve this organization which had been built up with almost fifty years of unremitting toil. I have no doubt that no self-respecting White political organization would disband itself if declared illegal by a government in which it had no say.

In 1960 the Government held a referendum which led to the establishment of the Republic. Africans, who constituted approximately 70 per cent of the population of South Africa, were not entitled to vote, and were not even consulted about the proposed constitutional change. All of us were apprehensive of our future under the proposed White Republic, and a resolution was taken to hold an All-In African Conference to call for a National Convention, and to organize mass demonstrations on the eve of the unwanted Republic, if the Government failed to call the Convention. The conference was attended by Africans of various political persuasions. I was the Secretary of the conference and undertook to be responsible for organizing the national stay-at-home which was subsequently called to coincide with the declaration of the Republic. As all strikes by Africans are illegal, the person organizing such a strike must avoid arrest. I was chosen to be this person, and consequently I had to leave my home and family and my practice and go into hiding to avoid arrest.

The stay-at-home, in accordance with ANC policy, was to be a peaceful demonstration. Careful instructions were given to organizers and members to avoid any recourse to violence. The Government's answer was to introduce new and harsher laws, to mobilize its armed forces, and to send Saracens, armed vehicles, and soldiers into the townships in a massive show of force designed to intimidate the people. This was an indication that the Government had decided to rule by force alone, and this decision was a milestone on the road to Umkhonto.

Some of this may appear irrelevant to this trial. In fact, I believe none of it is irrelevant because it will, I hope, enable the Court to appreciate the attitude eventually adopted by the various persons and bodies concerned in the National Liberation Movement. When I went to jail in 1962, the dominant idea was that loss of life should be avoided. I now know that this was still so in 1963.

I must return to June 1961. What were we, the leaders of our people, to do? Were we to give in to the show of force and the implied threat against future action, or were we to fight it and, if so, how?

We had no doubt that we had to continue the fight. Anything else would have been abject surrender. Our problem was not whether to fight, but was how to continue the fight. We of the ANC had always stood for a non-racial democracy, and we shrank from any action which might drive the races further apart than they already were. But the hard facts were that fifty years of non-violence had brought the African people nothing but more and more repressive legislation, and fewer and fewer rights. It may not be easy for this Court to understand, but it is a fact that for a long time the people had been talking of violence — of the day when they would fight the White man and win back their country — and we, the leaders of the ANC, had nevertheless always prevailed upon them to avoid violence and to pursue peaceful methods. When some of us discussed this in May and June of 1961, it could not be denied that our policy to achieve a nonracial State by non-violence had achieved nothing, and that our followers were beginning to lose confidence in this policy and were developing disturbing ideas of terrorism.

It must not be forgotten that by this time violence had, in fact, become a feature of the South African political scene. There had been violence in 1957 when the women of Zeerust were ordered to carry passes; there was violence in 1958 with the enforcement of cattle culling in Sekhukhuniland; there was violence in 1959 when the people of Cato Manor protested against pass raids; there was violence in 1960 when the Government attempted to impose Bantu Authorities in Pondoland. Thirty-nine Africans died in these disturbances. In 1961 there had been riots in Warmbaths, and all this time the Transkei had been a seething mass of unrest. Each disturbance pointed clearly to the inevitable growth among Africans of the belief that violence was the only way out — it showed that a Government which uses force to maintain its rule teaches the oppressed to use force to oppose it. Already small groups had arisen in the urban areas and were spontaneously making plans for violent forms of political struggle. There now arose a danger that these groups would adopt terrorism against Africans, as well as Whites, if not properly directed. Particularly disturbing was the type of violence engendered in places such as Zeerust, Sekhukhuniland, and Pondoland amongst Africans. It was increasingly taking the form, not of struggle against the Government—though this is what prompted it—but of civil strife amongst themselves, conducted in such a way that it could not hope to achieve anything other than a loss of life and bitterness.

At the beginning of June 1961, after a long and anxious assessment of the South African situation, I, and some colleagues, came to the conclusion that as violence in this country was inevitable, it would be unrealistic and wrong for African leaders to continue preaching peace and non-violence at a time when the Government met our peaceful demands with force.

This conclusion was not easily arrived at. It was only when all else had failed, when all channels of peaceful protest had been barred to us, that the decision was made to embark on violent forms of political struggle, and to form Umkhonto we Sizwe. We did so not because we desired such a course, but solely because the Government had left us with no other choice. In the Manifesto of Umkhonto published on 16 December 1961, which is Exhibit AD, we said:

"The time comes in the life of any nation when there remain only two choices—submit or fight. That time has now come to South Africa. We shall not submit and we have no choice but to hit back by all means in our power in defence of our people, our future, and our freedom".

This was our feeling in June of 1961 when we decided to press for a change in the policy of the National Liberation Movement. I can only say that I felt morally obliged to do what I did.

We who had taken this decision started to consult leaders of various organizations, including the ANC. I will not say whom we spoke to, or what they said, but I wish to deal with the role of the African National Congress in this phase of the struggle, and with the policy and objectives of Umkhonto we Sizwe.

As far as the ANC was concerned, it formed a clear view, which can be summarized as follows:

It was a mass political organization with a political function to fulfill. Its members had joined on the express policy of non-violence.

Because of all this, it could not and would not undertake violence. This must be stressed. One cannot turn such a body into the small, closely knit organization required for sabotage. Nor would this be politically correct, because it would result in members ceasing to carry out this essential activity: political propaganda and organization. Nor was it permissible to change the whole nature of the organization.

On the other hand, in view of this situation I have described, the ANC was prepared to depart from its fifty-year-old policy of non-violence to this extent that it would no longer disapprove of properly controlled violence. Hence members who undertook such activity would not be subject to disciplinary action by the ANC.

I say "properly controlled violence" because I made it clear that if I formed the organization I would at all times subject it to the political guidance of the ANC and would not undertake any different form of activity from that contemplated without the consent of the ANC. And I shall now tell the Court how that form of violence came to be determined.

As a result of this decision, Umkhonto was formed in November 1961. When we took this decision, and subsequently formulated our plans, the ANC heritage of non-violence and racial harmony was very much with us. We felt that the country was drifting towards a civil war in which Blacks and Whites would fight each other. We viewed the situation with alarm. Civil war could mean the destruction of what the ANC stood for; with civil war, racial peace would be more difficult than ever to achieve. We already have examples in South African history of the results of war. It has taken more than fifty years for the scars of the South African War to disappear. How much longer would it take to eradicate the scars of inter-racial civil war, which could not be fought without a great loss of life on both sides?

The avoidance of civil war had dominated our thinking for many years, but when we decided to adopt violence as part of our policy, we realized that we might one day have to face the prospect of such a war. This had to be taken into account in formulating our plans. We required a plan which was flexible and which permitted us to act in accordance with the needs of the times; above all, the plan had to be one which recognized civil war as the last resort, and left the decision on this question to the future. We did not want to be committed to civil war, but we wanted to be ready if it became inevitable.

Four forms of violence were possible. There is sabotage, there is guerrilla warfare, there is terrorism, and there is open revolution. We chose to adopt the first method and to exhaust it before taking any other decision.

In the light of our political background the choice was a logical one. Sabotage did not involve loss of life, and it offered the best hope for future race relations. Bitterness would be kept to a minimum and, if the policy bore fruit, democratic government could become a reality. This is what we felt at the time, and this is what we said in our Manifesto (Exhibit AD):

"We of Umkhonto we Sizwe have always sought to achieve liberation without bloodshed and civil clash. We hope, even at this late hour, that our first actions will awaken everyone to a realization of the disastrous situation to which the Nationalist policy is leading. We hope that we will bring the Government and its supporters to their senses before it is too late, so that both the Government and its policies can be changed before matters reach the desperate state of civil war."

The initial plan was based on a careful analysis of the political and economic situation of our country. We believed that South Africa depended to a large extent on foreign capital and foreign trade. We felt that planned destruction of power plants, and interference with rail and telephone communications, would tend to scare away capital from the country, make it more difficult for goods from the industrial areas to reach the seaports on schedule, and would in the long run be a heavy drain on the economic life of the country, thus compelling the voters of the country to reconsider their position.

Attacks on the economic life lines of the country were to be linked with sabotage on Government buildings and other symbols of apartheid. These attacks would serve as a source of inspiration to our people. In addition, they would provide an outlet for those people who were urging the adoption of violent methods and would enable us to give concrete proof to our followers that we had adopted a stronger line and were fighting back against Government violence.

In addition, if mass action were successfully organized, and mass reprisals taken, we felt that sympathy for our cause would be roused in other countries, and that greater pressure would be brought to bear on the South African Government.

This then was the plan. Umkhonto was to perform sabotage, and strict instructions were given to its members right from the start, that on no account were they to injure or kill people in planning or carrying out operations. These instructions have been referred to in the evidence of "Mr. X" and "Mr. Z".

The affairs of the Umkhonto were controlled and directed by a National High Command, which had powers of co-option and which could, and did, appoint Regional Commands. The High Command was the body which determined tactics and targets and was in charge of training and finance. Under the High Command there were Regional Commands which were responsible for the direction of the local sabotage groups. Within the framework of the policy laid down by the National High Command, the Regional Commands had authority to select the targets to be attacked. They had no authority to go beyond the prescribed framework and thus had no authority to embark upon acts which endangered life, or which did not fit into the overall plan of sabotage. For instance, Umkhonto members were forbidden ever to go armed into operation.

Incidentally, the terms High Command and Regional Command were an importation from the Jewish national underground organization Irgun Zvai Leumi, which operated in Israel between 1944 and 1948.

Umkhonto had its first operation on 16 December 1961, when Government buildings in Johannesburg, Port Elizabeth and Durban were attacked. The selection of targets is proof of the policy to which I have referred. Had we intended to attack life we would have selected targets where people congregated and not empty buildings and power stations. The sabotage which was committed before 16 December 1961 was the work of isolated groups and had no connection whatever with Umkhonto. In fact, some of these and a number of later acts were claimed by other organizations.

The Manifesto of Umkhonto was issued on the day that operations commenced. The response to our actions and Manifesto among the white population was characteristically violent. The Government threatened to take strong action, and called upon its supporters to stand firm and to ignore the demands of the Africans. The Whites failed to respond by suggesting change; they responded to our call by suggesting the laager.

In contrast, the response of the Africans was one of encouragement. Suddenly there was hope again. Things were happening. People in the townships became eager for political news. A great deal of enthusiasm was generated by the initial successes, and people began to speculate on how soon freedom would be obtained.

But we in Umkhonto weighed up the white response with anxiety. The lines were being drawn. The whites and blacks were moving into separate camps, and the prospects of avoiding a civil war were made less. The white newspapers carried reports that sabotage would be punished by death. If this was so, how could we continue to keep Africans away from terrorism?

Already scores of Africans had died as a result of racial friction. In 1920 when the famous leader, Masabala, was held in

Port Elizabeth jail, twenty-four of a group of Africans who had gathered to demand his release were killed by the police and white civilians. In 1921, more than one hundred Africans died in the Bulhoek affair. In 1924 over two hundred Africans were killed when the Administrator of South-West Africa led a force against a group which had rebelled against the imposition of dog tax. On 1 May 1950, eighteen Africans died as a result of police shootings during the strike. On 21 March 1960, sixty-nine unarmed Africans died at Sharpeville.

How many more Sharpevilles would there be in the history of our country? And how many more Sharpevilles could the country stand without violence and terror becoming the order of the day? And what would happen to our people when that stage was reached? In the long run we felt certain we must succeed, but at what cost to ourselves and the rest of the country? And if this happened, how could black and white ever live together again in peace and harmony? These were the problems that faced us, and these were our decisions.

Experience convinced us that rebellion would offer the Government limitless opportunities for the indiscriminate slaughter of our people. But it was precisely because the soil of South Africa is already drenched with the blood of innocent Africans that we felt it our duty to make preparations as a long-term undertaking to use force in order to defend ourselves against force. If war were inevitable, we wanted the fight to be conducted on terms most favourable to our people. The fight which held out prospects best for us and the least risk of life to both sides was guerrilla warfare. We decided, therefore, in our preparations for the future, to make provision for the possibility of guerrilla warfare.

All whites undergo compulsory military training, but no such training was given to Africans. It was in our view essential to build up a nucleus of trained men who would be able to provide the leadership which would be required if guerrilla warfare started. We had to prepare for such a situation before it became too late to make proper preparations. It was also necessary to build up a nucleus of men trained in civil administration and other professions, so that Africans would be equipped to participate in the government of this country as soon as they were allowed to do so.

At this stage it was decided that I should attend the Conference of the Pan-African Freedom Movement for Central, East, and Southern Africa, which was to be held early in 1962 in Addis Ababa, and, because of our need for preparation, it was also decided that, after the conference, I would undertake a tour of the African States with a view to obtaining facilities for the training of soldiers, and that I would also solicit scholarships for the higher education of matriculated Africans. Training in both fields would be necessary, even if changes came about by peaceful means. Administrators would be necessary who would be willing and able to administer a non-racial State and so would men be necessary to control the army and police force of such a State.

It was on this note that I left South Africa to proceed to Addis Ababa as a delegate of the ANC. My tour was a success. Wherever I went I met sympathy for our cause and promises of help. All Africa was united against the stand of White South Africa, and even in London I was received with great sympathy by political leaders, such as Mr. Gaitskell and Mr. Grimond. In Africa I was promised support by such men as Julius Nyerere, now President of Tanganyika; Mr. Kawawa, then Prime Minister of Tanganyika; Emperor Haile Selassie of Ethiopia; General Abboud, President of the Sudan; Habib Bourguiba, President of Tunisia; Ben Bella, now President of Algeria; Modibo Keita, President of Mali; Leopold Senghor, President of Senegal; Sekou Toure, President of Guinea; President Tubman of Liberia; and Milton Obote, Prime Minister of Uganda. It was Ben Bella who invited me to visit Oujda, the Headquarters of the Algerian Army of National Liberation, the visit which is described in my diary, one of the Exhibits.

I started to make a study of the art of war and revolution and, whilst abroad, underwent a course in military training. If there was to be guerrilla warfare, I wanted to be able to stand and fight with my people and to share the hazards of war with them. Notes of lectures which I received in Algeria are contained in Exhibit 16, produced in evidence. Summaries of books on guerrilla warfare and military strategy have also been produced. I have already admitted that these documents are in my writing, and I acknowledge that I made these studies to equip myself for the role which I might have to play if the struggle drifted into guerrilla warfare. I approached this question as every African Nationalist should do. I was completely objective. The Court will see that I attempted to examine all types of authority on the subject—from the East and from the West, going back to the classic work of Clausewitz, and covering such a variety as Mao Tse Tung and Che Guevara on the one hand, and the writings on the Anglo-Boer War on the other. Of course, these notes are merely summaries of the books I read and do not contain my personal views.

I also made arrangements for our recruits to undergo military training. But here it was impossible to organize any scheme without the co-operation of the ANC offices in Africa. I consequently obtained the permission of the ANC in South Africa to do this. To this extent then there was a departure from the original decision of the ANC, but it applied outside South Africa only. The first batch of recruits actually arrived in Tanganyika when I was passing through that country on my way back to South Africa.

I returned to South Africa and reported to my colleagues on the results of my trip. On my return I found that there had been little alteration in the political scene save that the threat of a death penalty for sabotage had now become a fact. The attitude of my colleagues in Umkhonto was much the same as it had been before I left. They were feeling their way cautiously and felt that it would be a long time before the possibilities of sabotage were exhausted. In fact, the view was expressed by some that the training of recruits was premature. This is recorded by me in the document which is Exhibit R.14. After a full discussion, however, it was decided to go ahead with the plans for military training because of the fact that it would take many years to build up a sufficient nucleus of trained soldiers to start a guerrilla campaign, and whatever happened the training would be of value.

I wish to turn now to certain general allegations made in this case by the State. But before doing so, I wish to revert to certain occurrences said by witnesses to have happened in Port Elizabeth and East London. I am referring to the bombing of private houses of pro-Government persons during September, October and November 1962. I do not know what justification there was for these acts, nor what provocation had been given. But if what I have said already is accepted, then it is clear that these acts had nothing to do with the carrying out of the policy of Umkhonto.

One of the chief allegations in the indictment is that the ANC was a party to a general conspiracy to commit sabotage. I have already explained why this is incorrect but how, externally, there was a departure from the original principle laid down by the ANC. There has, of course, been overlapping of functions internally as well, because there is a difference between a resolution adopted in the atmosphere of a committee room and the concrete difficulties that arise in the field of practical activity. At a later stage the position was further affected by bannings and house arrests, and by persons leaving the country to take up political work abroad. This led to individuals having to do work in different capacities. But though this may have blurred the distinction between Umkhonto and the ANC, it by no means abolished that distinction. Great care was taken to keep the activities of the two organizations in South Africa distinct. The ANC remained a mass political body of Africans only carrying on the type of political work they had conducted prior to 1961. Umkhonto remained a small organization recruiting its members from different races and organizations and trying to achieve its own particular object. The fact that members of Umkhonto were recruited from the ANC, and the fact that persons served both organizations, like Solomon Mbanjwa, did not, in our view, change the nature of the ANC or give it a policy of violence. This overlapping of officers, however, was more the exception than the rule. This is why persons such as "Mr. X" and "Mr. Z", who were on the Regional Command of their respective areas, did not participate in any of the ANC committees or activities, and why people such as Mr. Bennett Mashiyana and Mr. Reginald Ndubi did not hear of sabotage at their ANC meetings.

Another of the allegations in the indictment is that Rivonia was the headquarters of Umkhonto. This is not true of the time when I was there. I was told, of course, and knew that certain of the activities of the Communist Party were carried on there. But this is no reason (as I shall presently explain) why I should not use the place.

I came there in the following manner:

As already indicated, early in April 1961 I went underground to organize the May general strike. My work entailed traveling throughout the country, living now in African townships, then in country villages and again in cities.

During the second half of the year I started visiting the Parktown home of Arthur Goldreich, where I used to meet my family privately. Although I had no direct political association with him, I had known Arthur Goldreich socially since 1958.

In October, Arthur Goldreich informed me that he was moving out of town and offered me a hiding place there. A few days thereafter, he arranged for Michael Harmel to take me to Rivonia. I naturally found Rivonia an ideal place for the man who lived the life of an outlaw. Up to that time I had been compelled to live indoors during the daytime and could only venture out under cover of darkness. But at Liliesleaf I could live differently and work far more efficiently.

For obvious reasons, I had to disguise myself and I assumed the fictitious name of David. In December, Arthur Goldreich and his family moved in. I stayed there until I went abroad on 11 January 1962. As already indicated, I returned in July 1962 and was arrested in Natal on 5 August.

Up to the time of my arrest, Liliesleaf farm was the headquarters of neither the African National Congress nor Umkhonto. With the exception of myself, none of the officials or members of these bodies lived there, no meetings of the governing bodies were ever held there, and no activities connected with them were either organized or directed from there. On numerous occasions during my stay at Liliesleaf farm I met both the Executive Committee of the ANC, as well as the NHC, but such meetings were held elsewhere and not on the farm.

Whilst staying at Liliesleaf farm, I frequently visited Arthur Goldreich in the main house and he also paid me visits in my room. We had numerous political discussions covering a variety of subjects. We discussed ideological and practical questions, the Congress Alliance, Umkhonto and its activities generally, and his experiences as a soldier in the Palmach, the military wing of the Haganah. Haganah was the political authority of the Jewish National Movement in Palestine.

Because of what I had got to know of Goldreich, I recommended on my return to South Africa that he should be recruited to Umkhonto. I do not know of my personal knowledge whether this was done.

Another of the allegations made by the State is that the aims and objects of the ANC and the Communist Party are the same. I wish to deal with this and with my own political position, because I must assume that the State may try to argue from certain Exhibits that I tried to introduce Marxism into the ANC. The allegation as to the ANC is false. This is an old allegation which was disproved at the Treason Trial and which has again reared its head. But since the allegation has been made again, I shall deal with it as well as with the relationship between the ANC and the Communist Party and Umkhonto and that party.

The ideological creed of the ANC is, and always has been, the creed of African Nationalism. It is not the concept of African Nationalism expressed in the cry, "Drive the White man into the sea". The African Nationalism for which the ANC stands is the concept of freedom and fulfillment for the African people in their own land. The most important political document ever adopted by the ANC is the "Freedom Charter". It is by no means a blueprint for a socialist state. It calls for redistribution, but not nationalization, of land; it provides for nationalization of mines, banks, and monopoly industry, because big monopolies are owned by one race only, and without such nationalization racial domination would be perpetuated despite the spread of political power. It would be a hollow gesture to repeal the Gold Law prohibitions against Africans when all gold mines are owned by European companies. In this respect the ANC's policy corresponds with the old policy of the present Nationalist Party, which, for many years, had as part of its programme the nationalization of the gold mines which, at that time, were controlled by foreign capital. Under the Freedom Charter, nationalization would take place in an economy based on private enterprise. The realization of the Freedom Charter would open up fresh fields for a prosperous African population of all classes, including the middle class. The ANC has never at any period of its history advocated a revolutionary change in the economic structure of the country, nor has it, to the best of my recollection, ever condemned capitalist society.

As far as the Communist Party is concerned, and if I understand its policy correctly, it stands for the establishment of a State based on the principles of Marxism. Although it is prepared to work for the Freedom Charter, as a short term solution to the problems created by white supremacy, it regards the Freedom Charter as the beginning, and not the end, of its programme.

The ANC, unlike the Communist Party, admitted Africans only as members. Its chief goal was, and is, for the African people to win unity and full political rights. The Communist Party's main aim, on the other hand, was to remove the capitalists and to replace them with a working-class government. The Communist Party sought to emphasize class distinctions whilst the ANC seeks to harmonize them. This is a vital distinction.

It is true that there has often been close co-operation between the ANC and the Communist Party. But co-operation is merely proof of a common goal — in this case the removal of white supremacy — and is not proof of a complete community of interests.

The history of the world is full of similar examples. Perhaps the most striking illustration is to be found in the co-operation between Great Britain, the United States of America, and the Soviet Union in the fight against Hitler. Nobody but Hitler would have dared to suggest that such co-operation turned Churchill or Roosevelt into communists or communist tools, or that Britain and America were working to bring about a communist world.

Another instance of such co-operation is to be found precisely in Umkhonto. Shortly after Umkhonto was constituted, I was informed by some of its members that the Communist Party would support Umkhonto, and this then occurred. At a later stage the support was made openly.

I believe that communists have always played an active role in the fight by colonial countries for their freedom, because the short-term objects of communism would always correspond with the long-term objects of freedom movements. Thus communists have played an important role in the freedom struggles fought in countries such as Malaya, Algeria, and Indonesia, yet none of these States today are communist countries. Similarly in the underground resistance movements which sprung up in Europe during the last World War, communists played an important role. Even General Chiang Kai-Shek, today one of the bitterest enemies of communism, fought together with the communists against the ruling class in the struggle which led to his assumption of power in China in the 1930s.

This pattern of co-operation between communists and non-communists has been repeated in the National Liberation Movement of South Africa. Prior to the banning of the Communist Party, joint campaigns involving the Communist Party and the Congress movements were accepted practice. African communists could, and did, become members of the ANC, and some served on the National, Provincial, and local committees. Amongst those who served on the National

Executive are Albert Nzula, a former Secretary of the Communist Party, Moses Kotane, another former Secretary, and J. B. Marks, a former member of the Central Committee.

I joined the ANC in 1944, and in my younger days I held the view that the policy of admitting communists to the ANC, and the close co-operation which existed at times on specific issues between the ANC and the Communist Party, would lead to a watering down of the concept of African Nationalism. At that stage I was a member of the African National Congress Youth League, and was one of a group which moved for the expulsion of communists from the ANC. This proposal was heavily defeated. Amongst those who voted against the proposal were some of the most conservative sections of African political opinion. They defended the policy on the ground that from its inception the ANC was formed and built up, not as a political party with one school of political thought, but as a Parliament of the African people, accommodating people of various political convictions, all united by the common goal of national liberation. I was eventually won over to this point of view and I have upheld it ever since.

It is perhaps difficult for white South Africans, with an ingrained prejudice against communism, to understand why experienced African politicians so readily accept communists as their friends. But to us the reason is obvious. Theoretical differences amongst those fighting against oppression is a luxury we cannot afford at this stage. What is more, for many decades communists were the only political group in South Africa who were prepared to treat Africans as human beings and their equals; who were prepared to eat with us; talk with us, live with us, and work with us. They were the only political group which was prepared to work with the Africans for the attainment of political rights and a stake in society. Because of this, there are many Africans who, today, tend to equate freedom with communism. They are supported in this belief by a legislature which brands all exponents of democratic government and African freedom as communists and bans many of them (who are not communists) under the Suppression of Communism Act. Although I have never been a member of the Communist Party, I myself have been named under that pernicious Act because of the role I played in the Defiance Campaign. I have also been banned and imprisoned under that Act.

It is not only in internal politics that we count communists as amongst those who support our cause. In the international field, communist countries have always come to our aid. In the United Nations and other Councils of the world the communist bloc has supported the Afro-Asian struggle against colonialism and often seems to be more sympathetic to our plight than some of the Western powers. Although there is a universal condemnation of apartheid, the communist bloc speaks out against it with a louder voice than most of the white world. In these circumstances, it would take a brash young politician, such as I was in 1949, to proclaim that the Communists are our enemies.

I turn now to my own position. I have denied that I am a communist, and I think that in the circumstances I am obliged to state exactly what my political beliefs are.

I have always regarded myself, in the first place, as an African patriot. After all, I was born in Umtata, forty-six years ago. My guardian was my cousin, who was the acting paramount chief of Tembuland, and I am related both to the present paramount chief of Tembuland, Sabata Dalindyebo, and to Kaizer Matanzima, the Chief Minister of the Transkei.

Today I am attracted by the idea of a classless society, an attraction which springs in part from Marxist reading and, in part, from my admiration of the structure and organization of early African societies in this country. The land, then the main means of production, belonged to the tribe. There were no rich or poor and there was no exploitation.

It is true, as I have already stated, that I have been influenced by Marxist thought. But this is also true of many of the leaders of the new independent States. Such widely different persons as Gandhi, Nehru, Nkrumah, and Nasser all acknowledge this fact. We all accept the need for some form of socialism to enable our people to catch up with the advanced countries of this world and to overcome their legacy of extreme poverty. But this does not mean we are Marxists.

Indeed, for my own part, I believe that it is open to debate whether the Communist Party has any specific role to play at this particular stage of our political struggle. The basic task at the present moment is the removal of race discrimination and the attainment of democratic rights on the basis of the Freedom Charter. In so far as that Party furthers this task, I welcome its assistance. I realize that it is one of the means by which people of all races can be drawn into our struggle.

From my reading of Marxist literature and from conversations with Marxists, I have gained the impression that communists regard the parliamentary system of the West as undemocratic and reactionary. But, on the contrary, I am an admirer of such a system.

The Magna Carta, the Petition of Rights, and the Bill of Rights are documents which are held in veneration by democrats throughout the world.

I have great respect for British political institutions, and for the country's system of justice. I regard the British Parliament as the most democratic institution in the world, and the independence and impartiality of its judiciary never fail to arouse my admiration.

The American Congress, that country's doctrine of separation of powers, as well as the independence of its judiciary, arouses in me similar sentiments.

I have been influenced in my thinking by both West and East. All this has led me to feel that in my search for a political formula, I should be absolutely impartial and objective. I should tie myself to no particular system of society other than of socialism. I must leave myself free to borrow the best from the West and from the East . . .

There are certain Exhibits which suggest that we received financial support from abroad, and I wish to deal with this question.

Our political struggle has always been financed from internal sources—from funds raised by our own people and by our own supporters. Whenever we had a special campaign or an important political case—for example, the Treason Trial—we received financial assistance from sympathetic individuals and organizations in the Western countries. We had never felt it necessary to go beyond these sources.

But when in 1961 the Umkhonto was formed, and a new phase of struggle introduced, we realized that these events would make a heavy call on our slender resources, and that the scale of our activities would be hampered by the lack of funds. One of my instructions, as I went abroad in January 1962, was to raise funds from the African states.

I must add that, whilst abroad, I had discussions with leaders of political movements in Africa and discovered that almost every single one of them, in areas which had still not attained independence, had received all forms of assistance from the socialist countries, as well as from the West, including that of financial support. I also discovered that some well-known African states, all of them non-communists, and even anti-communists, had received similar assistance.

On my return to the Republic, I made a strong recommendation to the ANC that we should not confine ourselves to Africa and the Western countries, but that we should also send a mission to the socialist countries to raise the funds which we so urgently needed.

I have been told that after I was convicted such a mission was sent, but I am not prepared to name any countries to which it went, nor am I at liberty to disclose the names of the organizations and countries which gave us support or promised to do so.

As I understand the State case, and in particular the evidence of "Mr. X", the suggestion is that Umkhonto was the inspiration of the Communist Party which sought by playing upon imaginary grievances to enroll the African people into an army which ostensibly was to fight for African freedom, but in reality was fighting for a communist state. Nothing could be further from the truth. In fact the suggestion is preposterous. Umkhonto was formed by Africans to further their struggle for freedom in their own land. Communists and others supported the movement, and we only wish that more sections of the community would join us.

Our fight is against real, and not imaginary, hardships or, to use the language of the State Prosecutor, "so-called hardships". Basically, we fight against two features which are the hallmarks of African life in South Africa and which are entrenched by legislation which we seek to have repealed. These features are poverty and lack of human dignity, and we do not need communists or so-called "agitators" to teach us about these things.

South Africa is the richest country in Africa, and could be one of the richest countries in the world. But it is a land of extremes and remarkable contrasts. The whites enjoy what may well be the highest standard of living in the world, whilst Africans live in poverty and misery. Forty per cent of the Africans live in hopelessly overcrowded and, in some cases, drought-stricken Reserves, where soil erosion and the overworking of the soil makes it impossible for them to live properly off the land. Thirty per cent are labourers, labour tenants, and squatters on white farms and work and live under conditions similar to those of the serfs of the Middle Ages. The other 30 per cent live in towns where they have developed economic and social habits which bring them closer in many respects to white standards. Yet most Africans, even in this group, are impoverished by low incomes and high cost of living.

The highest-paid and the most prosperous section of urban African life is in Johannesburg. Yet their actual position is desperate. The latest figures were given on 25 March 1964 by Mr. Carr, Manager of the Johannesburg Non-European Affairs Department. The poverty datum line for the average African family in Johannesburg (according to Mr. Carr's department) is R42.84 per month. He showed that the average monthly wage is

R32.24 and that 46 per cent of all African families in Johannesburg do not earn enough to keep them going.

Poverty goes hand in hand with malnutrition and disease. The incidence of malnutrition and deficiency diseases is very high amongst Africans. Tuberculosis, pellagra, kwashiorkor, gastro-enteritis, and scurvy bring death and destruction of health. The incidence of infant mortality is one of the highest in the world. According to the Medical Officer of Health for Pretoria, tuberculosis kills forty people a day (almost all Africans), and in 1961 there were 58,491 new cases reported. These diseases not only destroy the vital organs of the body, but they result in retarded mental conditions and lack of initiative, and reduce powers of concentration. The secondary results of such conditions affect the whole community and the standard of work performed by African labourers.

The complaint of Africans, however, is not only that they are poor and the whites are rich, but that the laws which are made by the whites are designed to preserve this situation. There are two ways to break out of poverty. The first is by formal education, and the second is by the worker acquiring a greater skill at his work and thus higher wages. As far as Africans are concerned, both these avenues of advancement are deliberately curtailed by legislation.

The present Government has always sought to hamper Africans in their search for education. One of their early acts, after coming into power, was to stop subsidies for African school feeding. Many African children who attended schools depended on this supplement to their diet. This was a cruel act.

There is compulsory education for all white children at virtually no cost to their parents, be they rich or poor. Similar facilities are not provided for the African children, though there are some who receive such assistance. African children, however, generally have to pay more for their schooling than whites. According to figures quoted by the South African Institute of Race Relations in its 1963 journal, approximately 40 per cent of African children in the age group between seven to fourteen do not attend school. For those who do attend school, the standards are vastly different from those afforded to white children. In 1960-61 the per capita Government spending on African students at State-aided schools was estimated at R12.46. In the same years, the per capita spending on white children in the Cape Province (which are the only figures available to me) was R144.57. Although there are no figures available to me, it can be stated, without doubt, that the white children on whom R144.57 per head was being spent all came from wealthier homes than African children on whom R12.46 per head was being spent.

The quality of education is also different. According to the Bantu Educational Journal, only 5,660 African children in the whole of South Africa passed their Junior Certificate in 1962, and in that year only 362 passed matric. This is presumably consistent with the policy of Bantu education about which the present Prime Minister said, during the debate on the Bantu Education Bill in 1953:

"When I have control of Native education I will reform it so that Natives will be taught from childhood to realize that equality with Europeans is not for them . . . People who believe in equality are not desirable teachers for Natives. When my Department controls Native education it will know for what class of higher education a Native is fitted, and whether he will have a chance in life to use his knowledge."

The other main obstacle to the economic advancement of the African is the industrial colour-bar under which all the better jobs of industry are reserved for Whites only. Moreover, Africans who do obtain employment in the unskilled and semi-skilled occupations which are open to them are not allowed to form trade unions which have recognition under the Industrial Conciliation Act. This means that strikes of African workers are illegal, and that they are denied the right of collective bargaining which is permitted to the better-paid White workers. The discrimination in the policy of successive South African Governments towards African workers is demonstrated by the so-called "civilized labour policy" under which sheltered, unskilled Government jobs are found for those white workers who cannot make the grade in industry, at wages which far exceed the earnings of the average African employee in industry.

The Government often answers its critics by saying that Africans in South Africa are economically better off than the inhabitants of the other countries in Africa. I do not know whether this statement is true and doubt whether any comparison can be made without having regard to the cost-of-living index in such countries. But even if it is true, as far as the African people are concerned it is irrelevant. Our complaint is not that we are poor by comparison with people in other countries, but that we are poor by comparison with the white people in our own country, and that we are prevented by legislation from altering this imbalance.

The lack of human dignity experienced by Africans is the direct result of the policy of white supremacy. White supremacy implies black inferiority. Legislation designed to preserve white supremacy entrenches this notion. Menial tasks in South Africa are invariably performed by Africans. When anything has to be carried or cleaned the white man will look around for an African to do it for him, whether the African is employed by him or not. Because of this sort of attitude, whites tend to regard Africans as a separate breed. They do not look upon them as people with families of their own; they do not realize that they have emotions—that they fall in love like white people do; that they want to be with their wives and children like white people want to be with theirs; that they want to earn enough money to support their families properly, to feed and clothe them and send them to school. And what "house-boy" or "garden-boy" or labourer can ever hope to do this?

Pass laws, which to the Africans are among the most hated bits of legislation in South Africa, render any African liable to police surveillance at any time. I doubt whether there is a single African male in South Africa who has not at some stage had a brush with the police over his pass. Hundreds and thousands of Africans are thrown into jail each year under pass laws. Even worse than this is the fact that pass laws keep husband and wife apart and lead to the breakdown of family life.

Poverty and the breakdown of family life have secondary effects. Children wander about the streets of the townships because they have no schools to go to, or no money to enable them to go to school, or no parents at home to see that they go to school, because both parents (if there be two) have to work to keep the family alive. This leads to a breakdown in moral standards, to an alarming rise in illegitimacy, and to growing violence which erupts not only politically, but everywhere. Life in the townships is dangerous. There is not a day that goes by without somebody being stabbed or assaulted. And violence is carried out of the townships in the white living areas. People are afraid to walk alone in the streets after dark. Housebreakings and robberies are increasing, despite the fact that the death sentence can now be imposed for such offences. Death sentences cannot cure the festering sore.

Africans want to be paid a living wage. Africans want to perform work which they are capable of doing, and not work which the Government declares them to be capable of. Africans want to be allowed to live where they obtain work, and not be endorsed out of an area because they were not born there. Africans want to be allowed to own land in places where they work, and not to be obliged to live in rented houses which they can never call their own. Africans want to be part of the general population, and not confined to living in their own ghettoes. African men want to have their wives and children to live with them where they work, and not be forced into an unnatural existence in men's hostels. African women want to be with their menfolk and not be left permanently widowed in the Reserves. Africans want to be allowed out after eleven o'clock at night and not to be confined to their rooms like little children. Africans want to be allowed to travel in their own country and to seek work where they want to and not where the Labour Bureau tells them to. Africans want a just share in the whole of South Africa; they want security and a stake in society.

Above all, we want equal political rights, because without them our disabilities will be permanent. I know this sounds revolutionary to the whites in this country, because the majority of voters will be Africans. This makes the white man fear democracy.

But this fear cannot be allowed to stand in the way of the only solution which will guarantee racial harmony and freedom for all. It is not true that the enfranchisement of all will result in racial domination. Political division, based on colour, is entirely artificial and, when it disappears, so will the domination of one colour group by another. The ANC has spent half a century fighting against racialism. When it triumphs it will not change that policy.

This then is what the ANC is fighting. Their struggle is a truly national one. It is a struggle of the African people, inspired by their own suffering and their own experience. It is a struggle for the right to live.

During my lifetime I have dedicated myself to this struggle of the African people. I have fought against white domination, and I have fought against black domination. I have cherished the ideal of a democratic and free society in which all persons live together in harmony and with equal opportunities. It is an ideal which I hope to live for and to achieve. But if needs be, it is an ideal for which I am prepared to die.

Unite! Mobilise! Fight On!

1976

Between The Anvil Of United Mass Action And The Hammer Of The Armed Struggle We Shall Crush Apartheid!'

The African National Congress brings you this *urgent call to unity and mass action* by political prisoners on Robben Island to all patriots of our motherland. Nelson Mandela and hundreds of our comrades have been in the racist regime's prisons for more than 17 years. This message by Nelson Mandela addressed to the struggling masses of our country was written to deal with the present crisis gripping our enemy and in the aftermath of the Soweto uprisings. It was smuggled out of Robben Island prison under very difficult conditions and has taken over two years to reach us. None the less we believe the message remains fresh and valid and should be presented to our people. His call to unity and mass action is of particular importance in this Year of the Charter — 25th anniversary of the Freedom Charter. The ANC urges you to respond to this call and make 1980 a year of united mass struggle.

Oliver Tambo: President, ANC

Mandela's Call

Racists Rule By The Gun!

The gun has played an important part in our history. The resistance of the black man to white colonial intrusion was crushed by the gun. Our struggle to liberate ourselves from white domination is held in check by force of arms. From conquest to the present the story is the same. Successive white regimes have repeatedly massacred unarmed defenceless blacks. And wherever and whenever they have pulled out their guns the ferocity of their fire has been trained on the African people.

Apartheid is the embodiment of the racialism, repression and inhumanity of all previous white supremacist regimes. To see the real face of apartheid we must look beneath the veil of constitutional formulas, deceptive phrases and playing with words.

The rattle of gunfire and the rumbling of Hippo armoured vehicles since June 1976 have once again torn aside that veil. Spread across the face of our country, in black townships, the racist army and police have been pouring a hail of bullets killing and maiming hundreds of black men, women and children. The toll of the dead and injured already surpasses that of all past massacres carried out by this regime.

Apartheid is the rule of the gun and the hangman. The Hippo, the FN rifle and the gallows are its true symbols. These remain the easiest resort, the ever ready solution of the race-mad rulers of South Africa.

Vague Promises, Greater Repression . . .

In the midst of the present crisis, while our people count the dead and nurse the injured, they ask themselves: what lies ahead?

From our rulers we can expect nothing. They are the ones who give orders to the soldier crouching over his rifle: theirs is the spirit that moves the finger that caresses the trigger.

Vague promises, tinkerings with the machinery of apartheid, constitution juggling, massive arrests and detentions side by side with renewed overtures aimed at weakening and forestalling the unity of us blacks and dividing the forces of change—these are the fixed paths along which they will move. For they are neither capable nor willing to heed the verdict of the masses of our people.

The Verdict Of June 16!

That verdict is loud and clear: apartheid has failed. Our people remain unequivocal in its rejection. The young and the old, parent and child, all reject it. At the forefront of this 1976/77 wave of unrest were our students and youth. They come from the universities, high schools and even primary schools. They are a generation whose whole education has been under the diabolical design of the racists to poison the minds and brainwash our children into docile subjects of apartheid rule. But after more than twenty years of Bantu Education the circle is closed and nothing demonstrates the utter bankruptcy of apartheid as the revolt of our youth.

The evils, the cruelty and the inhumanity of apartheid have been there from its inception. And all blacks—Africans, Coloureds and Indians—have opposed it all along the line. What is now unmistakable, what the current wave of unrest has sharply highlighted, is this: that despite all the window-dressing and smooth talk, apartheid has become intolerable.

This awareness reaches over and beyond the particulars of our enslavement. The measure of this truth is the recognition by our people that under apartheid our lives, individually and collectively, count for nothing.

Unite!

We face an enemy that is deep-rooted, an enemy entrenched and determined not to yield. Our march to freedom is long and difficult. But both within and beyond our borders the prospects of victory grow bright.

The first condition for victory is black unity. Every effort to divide the blacks, to woo and pit one black group against another, must be vigorously repulsed. Our people — African, Coloured, Indian and democratic Whites — must be united into a single massive and solid wall of resistance, of united mass action.

Our struggle is growing sharper. This is not the time for the luxury of division and disunity. At all levels and in every walk of life we must close ranks. Within the ranks of the people differences must be submerged to the achievement of a single goal — the complete overthrow of apartheid and racist domination.

Victory Is Certain!

The revulsion of the world against apartheid is growing and the frontiers of white supremacy are shrinking. Mozambique and Angola are free and the war of liberation gathers force in Namibia and Zimbabwe. The soil of our country is destined to be the scene of the fiercest fight and the sharpest battles to rid our continent of the last vestiges of white minority rule.

The world is on our side. The OAU, the UN and the anti-apartheid movement continue to put pressure on the racist rulers of our country. Every effort to isolate South Africa adds strength to our struggle.

At all levels of our struggle, within and outside the country, much has been achieved and much remains to be done. But victory is certain!

We Salute All Of You!

We who are confined within the grey walls of the Pretoria regime's prisons reach out to our people. With you we count those who have perished by means of the gun and the hangman's rope. We salute all of you—the living, the injured and the dead. For you have dared to rise up against the tyrant's might.

Even as we bow at their graves we remember this: the dead live on as martyrs in our hearts and minds, a reproach to our disunity and the host of shortcomings that accompany divisions among the oppressed, a spur to our efforts to close ranks, and a reminder that the freedom of our people is yet to be won.

We face the future with confidence. For the guns that serve apartheid cannot render it unconquerable. Those who live by the gun shall perish by the gun.

Unite! Mobilise! Fight On!

Between the anvil of united mass action and the hammer of the armed struggle we shall crush apartheid and white minority racist rule.

Amandla Ngawethu! Matla Ke A Rona!

The Mandela Document

July 1989

The deepening political crisis in our country has been a matter of grave concern to me for quite some time and I now consider it necessary in the national interest for the African National Congress and the government to meet urgently to negotiate an effective political settlement.

At the outset I must point out that I make this move without consultation with the ANC. I am a loyal and disciplined member of the ANC, my political loyalty is owed, primarily, if not exclusively, to this organisation and particularly to our Lusaka headquarters where the official leadership is stationed and from where our affairs are directed.

The Organisation First

In the normal course of events, I would put my views to the organisation first, and if these views were accepted, the organisation would then decide on who were the best qualified members to handle the matter on its behalf and on exactly when to make the move. But in the current circumstances I cannot follow this course, and this is the only reason why I am acting on my own initiative, in the hope that the organisation will, in due course, endorse my action.

I must stress that no prisoner irrespective of his status or influence can conduct negotiations of this nature from prison. In our special situation negotiation on political matters is literally a matter of life and death which requires to be handled by the organisation itself through its appointed representatives.

The step I am taking should, therefore, not be seen as the beginning of actual negotiations between the government and the ANC. My task is a very limited one, and that is to bring the country's two major political bodies to the negotiating table.

My Release not the Issue

I must further point out that the question of my release from prison is not an issue, at least at this stage of the discussions, and I am certainly not asking to be freed. But I do hope that the government will, as soon as possible, give me the opportunity from my present quarters to sound the views of my colleagues inside and outside the country on this move. Only if this initiative is formally endorsed by the ANC will it have any significance.

I will touch presently on some of the problems which seem to constitute an obstacle to a meeting between the ANC and the government. But I must emphasize right at this stage that this step is not a response to the call by the government on ANC leaders to declare whether or not they are nationalists and to renounce the South African Communist Party before there can be negotiations. No self-respecting freedom fighter will take orders from the government on how to wage the freedom struggle against that same government and on who his allies in the freedom struggle should be.

To obey such instructions would be a violation of the long-standing and fruitful solidarity which distinguishes our liberation movement, and a betrayal of those who have worked so closely and suffered so much with us for almost 70 years. Far from responding to that call, my intervention is influenced by purely domestic issues, by the civil strife and ruin into which the country is now sliding. I am disturbed, as many other South Africans no doubt are, by the spectre of a South Africa split into two hostile camps; blacks (the term "blacks" is used in a broad sense to include all those who are not whites) on one side and whites on the other, slaughtering one another; by acute tensions which are building up dangerously in practically every sphere of our lives, a situation which, in turn, preshadows more violent clashes in the days ahead. This is the crisis that has freed me to act.

Current Views Among Blacks

I must add that the purpose of this discussion is not only to urge the government to talk to the ANC, but it is also to acquaint you with the views current among blacks, especially those in the Mass Democratic Movement.

If I am unable to express these views frankly and freely, you will never know how the majority of South Africans think on the policy and actions of the government; you will never know how to deal with their grievances and demands. It is perhaps proper to remind you that the media here and abroad has given certain public figures in this country a rather negative image not only in regard to human rights questions, but also in respect to their prescriptive stance when dealing with black leaders generally.

The impression is shared not only by the vast majority of blacks but also by a substantial section of the whites. If I had allowed myself to be influenced by this impression, I would not even have thought of making this move. Nevertheless, I have come here with an open mind and the impression I will carry away from this meeting will be determined almost exclusively by the manner in which you respond to my proposal.

It is in this spirit that I have undertaken this mission, and I sincerely hope that nothing will be done or said here that will force me to revise my views on this aspect.

Obstacles to Negotiation

I have already indicated that I propose to deal with some of the obstacles to a meeting between the government and the ANC. The government gives several reasons why it will not negotiate with us. However, for purposes of this discussion, I will confine myself to only three main demands set by the government as a precondition for negotiations, namely that the ANC must first renounce violence, break with the SACP, and abandon its demand for majority rule.

Renunciation of Violence

The position of the ANC on the question of violence is very simple. The organisation has no vested interest in violence. It abhors any action which may cause loss of life, destruction of property and misery to the people. It has worked long and patiently for a South Africa of common values and for an undivided and peaceful non-racial state. But we consider the armed struggle a legitimate form of self-defence against a morally repugnant system of government which will not allow even peaceful forms of protest.

It is more than ironical that it should be the government which demands that we should renounce violence. The government knows only too well that there is not a single political organisation in this country, inside and outside parliament, which can ever compare with the ANC in its total commitment to peaceful change.

Right from the early days of its history, the organisation diligently sought peaceful solutions and, to that extent, it talked patiently to successive South African governments, a policy we tried to follow in dealing with the present government.

Apartheid Violence

Not only did the government ignore our demands for a meeting, instead it took advantage of our commitment to a non-violent struggle and unleashed the most violent form of racial oppression this country has ever seen. It stripped us of all basic human rights, outlawed our organisations and barred all channels of peaceful resistance. It met our demands with force and, despite the grave problems facing the country, it continues to refuse to talk to us. There can only be one answer to this challenge; violent forms of struggle.

Down the years oppressed people have fought for their birthright by peaceful means, where that was possible, and through force where peaceful channels were closed. The history of this country also confirms this vital lesson. Africans as well as Afrikaners were, at one time or other, compelled to take up arms in defence of their freedom against British imperialism. The fact that both were finally defeated by superior arms, and by the vast resources of that empire, does not negate this lesson.

But from what has happened in South Africa during the last 40 years, we must conclude that now that the roles are reversed, and the Afrikaner is no longer a freedom fighter, but is in power, the entire lesson of history must be brushed aside. Not even a disciplined non-violent protest will now be tolerated. To the government a black man has neither a just cause to espouse nor freedom rights to defend. The whites must have the monopoly of political power, and of committing violence against innocent and defenceless people. That situation was totally unacceptable to us and the formation of *Umkhonto we Sizwe* was intended to end that monopoly, and to forcibly bring home to the government that the oppressed people of this country were prepared to stand up and defend themselves.

It is significant to note that throughout the past four decades, and more especially over the last 26 years, the government has met our demands with force only and has done hardly anything to create a suitable climate for dialogue. On the contrary, the government continues to govern with a heavy hand, and to incite whites against negotiation with the ANC. The publication of the booklet *Talking with the ANC*, which completely distorts the history and policy of the ANC, the extremely offensive language used by government spokesmen against freedom fighters, and the intimidation of whites who want to hear the views of the ANC at first hand, are all part of the government's strategy to wreck meaningful dialogue.

Pretoria Not Ready for Talks

It is perfectly clear on the facts that the refusal of the ANC to renounce violence is not the real problem facing the government. The truth is that the government is not yet ready for negotiation and for the sharing of political power with blacks. It is still committed to white domination and, for that reason, it will only tolerate those blacks who are willing to serve on its apartheid structures. Its policy is to remove from the political scene blacks who refuse to conform, who reject white supremacy and its apartheid structures, and who insist on equal rights with whites.

This is the real reason for the government's refusal to talk to us, and for its demand that we should disarm ourselves, while it continues to use violence against our people. This is the reason for its massive propaganda campaign to discredit the ANC, and present it to the public as a communist-dominated organisation bent on murder and destruction. In this situation the reaction of the oppressed people is clearly predictable.

Armed Struggle

White South Africa must accept the plain fact that the ANC will not suspend, to say nothing of abandoning, the armed struggle until the government shows its willingness to surrender the monopoly of political power, and to negotiate directly and in good faith with the acknowledged black leaders. The renunciation of violence by either the government or the

ANC should not be a precondition to, but the result of, negotiation.

Moreover, by ignoring credible black leaders, and imposing a succession of still-born negotiation structures, the government is not only squandering the country's precious resources but it is in fact discrediting the negotiation process itself, and prolonging civil strife. The position of the ANC on the question of violence is, therefore, very clear. A government which used violence against blacks many years before we took up arms has no right whatsoever to call on us to lay down arms.

The South African Communist Party

I have already pointed out that no self-respecting freedom fighter will allow the government to prescribe who his allies in the freedom struggle should be, and that to obey such instructions would be a betrayal of those who have suffered repression with us for so long.

We equally reject the charge that the ANC is dominated by the SACP and we regard the accusation as part of the smear campaign the government is waging against us. The accusation has, in effect, also been refuted by two totally independent sources. In January, 1987 the American State Department published a report on the activities of the SACP in this country which contrasts very sharply with the subjective picture the government has tried to paint against us over the years.

The essence of that report is that, although the influence of the SACP on the ANC is strong, it is unlikely that the Party will ever dominate the ANC.

The same point is made somewhat differently by Mr. Ismail Omar, member of the President's Council, in his book *Reform in Crisis* published in 1988, in which he gives concrete examples of important issues of the day over which the ANC and the SACP have differed.

He also points out that the ANC enjoys greater popular support than the SACP. He adds that, despite the many years of combined struggle, the two remain distinct organisations with ideological and policy differences which preclude a merger of identity.

These observations go some way towards disproving the accusation. But since the allegation has become the focal point of government propaganda against the ANC, I propose to use this opportunity to give you the correct information, in the hope that this will help you to see the matter in its proper perspective, and to evaluate your strategy afresh.

Co-operation between the ANC and the South African Communist Party goes back to the early 'twenties and has always been, and still is, strictly limited to the struggle against racial oppression and for a just society. At no time has the organisation ever adopted or co-operated with communism itself. Apart from the question of co-operation between the two organisations, members of the SACP have always been free to join the ANC. But once they do so, they become fully bound by the policy of the organisation set out in the Freedom Charter.

As members of the ANC engaged in the anti-apartheid struggle, their Marxist ideology is not directly relevant. The SACP has throughout the years accepted the leading role of the ANC, a position which is respected by the SACP members who join the ANC.

Firmly Established Tradition

There is, of course, a firmly established tradition in the ANC in terms of which any attempt is resisted, from whatever quarter, which is intended to undermine co-operation between the two organisations.

Even within the ranks of the ANC there have been, at one time or another, people—and some of them were highly respected and influential individuals—who were against this co-operation and who wanted SACP members expelled from the organisation. Those who persisted in these activities were themselves ultimately expelled or they broke away in despair.

In either case their departure ended their political careers, or they formed other political organisations which, in due course, crumbled into splinter groups. No dedicated ANC member will ever heed a call to break with the SACP. We regard such a demand as a purely divisive government strategy.

It is in fact a call on us to commit suicide. Which man of honour will ever desert a lifelong friend at the instance of a common opponent and still retain a measure of credibility among his people?

Which opponent will ever trust such a treacherous freedom fighter? Yet this is what the government is, in effect, asking us to do—to desert our faithful allies. We will not fall into that trap.

ANC is Non-Aligned

The government also accuses us of being agents of the Soviet Union. The truth is that the ANC is non-aligned, and we welcome support from the East and the West, from the socialist and capitalist countries. The only difference, as we have explained on countless occasions before, is that the socialist countries supply us with weapons, which the West refuses to give us. We have no intention whatsoever of changing our stand on this question.

The government's exaggerated hostility to the SACP and its refusal to have any dealings with that party have a hollow ring. Such an attitude is not only out of step with the growing co-operation between the capitalist and socialist countries in different parts of the world, but it is also inconsistent with the policy of the government itself, when dealing with our neighbouring states.

Not only has South Africa concluded treaties with the Marxist states of Angola and Mozambique—quite rightly in our opinion—but she also wants to strengthen ties with Marxist Zimbabwe. The government will certainly find it difficult, if not altogether impossible, to reconcile its readiness to work with foreign Marxists for the peaceful resolution of mutual problems, with its uncompromising refusal to talk to South African Marxists.

The reason for this inconsistency is obvious. As I have already said, the government is still too deeply committed to the principle of white domination and, despite lip service to reform, it is deadly opposed to the sharing of political power with blacks, and the SACP is merely being used as a smokescreen to retain the monopoly of political power.

The smear campaign against the ANC also helps the government to evade the real issue at stake, namely, the exclusion from political power of the black majority by a white minority, which is the source of all our troubles.

Personal Position

Concerning my own personal position, I have already informed you that I will not respond to the government's demand that ANC members should state whether they are members of the SACP or not.

But because much has been said by the media, as well as by government leaders regarding my political beliefs, I propose to use this opportunity to put the record straight.

My political beliefs have been explained in the course of several political trials in which I was charged, in the policy documents of the ANC and in my autobiography, *The Struggle is my Life*, which I wrote in prison in 1975.

I stated in these trials and publications that I did not belong to any organisation apart from the ANC. In my address to the court which sentenced me to life in prison in June 1964, I said:

"Today I am attracted by the idea of a classless society, an attraction which springs in part from Marxist reading, and in part from my admiration of the structure and organisation of early African societies in this country."

"It is true, as I have already stated, that I have been influenced by Marxist thought. But this is also true of many leaders of the new independent states. Such widely different persons as Gandhi, Nehru, Nkrumah and Nasser all acknowledge this fact. We all accept the need for some form of socialism to enable our people to catch up with the advanced countries of the world, and to overcome their legacy of poverty."

My Views Still the Same

My views are still the same. Equally important is the fact that many ANC leaders who are labeled communists by the government embrace nothing different from these beliefs. The term "communist" when used by the government has a totally different meaning from the conventional one. Practically every freedom fighter who receives his military training or education in the socialist countries is, to the government, a communist.

It would appear to be established government policy that, as long as the National Party is in power in this country, there can be no black freedom struggle, and no black freedom fighter. Any black political organisation which, like us, fights for the liberation of its people through armed struggle, must invariably be dominated by the SACP.

This attitude is not only the result of government propaganda. It is a logical consequence of white supremacy. After more than 300 years of racial indoctrination, the country's whites have developed such deep-seated contempt for blacks as to believe that we cannot think for ourselves, that we are incapable of fighting for political rights without incitement by some white agitator.

In accusing the ANC of domination by the SACP, and in calling on ANC members to renounce the Party, the government is deliberately exploiting that contempt.

Majority Rule

The government is equally vehement in condemning the principle of majority rule. The principle is rejected despite the fact that it is a pillar of democratic rule in many countries of the world. It is a principle which is fully accepted in the white politics of this country.

Only now that the stark reality has dawned that apartheid has failed, and that blacks will one day have an effective voice in government, are we told by whites here, and by their Western friends, that majority rule is a disaster to be avoided at all costs. Majority rule is acceptable to whites as long as it is considered within the context of white politics.

If black political aspirations are to be accommodated, then some other formula must be found provided that formula does not raise blacks to a position of equality with whites.

Yet majority rule and internal peace are like the two sides of a single coin, and white South Africa simply has to accept that there will never be peace and stability in this country until the principle is fully applied.

It is precisely because of its denial that the government has become the enemy of practically every black man. It is that denial that has sparked off the current civil strife.

Negotiated Political Settlement

By insisting on compliance with the above-mentioned conditions before there can be talks, the government clearly confirms that it wants no peace in this country but turmoil; no strong and independent ANC, but a weak and servile organisation playing a supportive role to white minority rule, not a non-aligned ANC but one which is a satellite of the West, and which is ready to serve the interests of capitalism.

No worthy leaders of a freedom movement will ever submit to conditions which are essentially terms of surrender dictated by a victorious commander to a beaten enemy, and which are really intended to weaken the organisation and to humiliate its leadership.

The key to the whole situation is a negotiated settlement, and a meeting between the government and the ANC will be the first major step towards lasting peace in the country, better relations with our neighbour states, admission to the Organisation of African Unity, readmission to the United Nations and other world bodies, to international markets and improved international relations generally.

An accord with the ANC, and the introduction of a non-racial society, is the only way in which our rich and beautiful country will be saved from the stigma which repels the world.

Two central issues will have to be addressed at such a meeting; firstly, the demand for majority rule in a unitary state; secondly, the concern of white South Africa over this demand, as well as the insistence of whites on structural guarantees that majority rule will not mean domination of the white minority by blacks.

The most crucial task which will face the government and the ANC will be to reconcile these two positions. Such reconciliation will be achieved only if both parties are willing to compromise. The organisation will determine precisely how negotiations should be conducted. It may well be that this should be done at least in two stages. The first, where the organisation and the government will work out together the preconditions for a proper climate for negotiations. Up to now both parties have been broadcasting their conditions for negotiations without putting them directly to each other.

The second stage would be the actual negotiations themselves when the climate is ripe for doing so. Any other approach would entail the danger of an irresolvable stalemate.

Overcome the Current Deadlock

Lastly, I must point out that the move I have taken provides you with the opportunity to overcome the current deadlock, and to normalise the country's political situation. I hope you will seize it without delay. I believe that the overwhelming majority of South Africans, black and white, hope to see the ANC and the government working closely together to lay the foundations for a new era in our country, in which racial discrimination and prejudice, coercion and confrontation death and destruction will be forgotten.

Mandela's Address After His Release From Prison

February 11, 1990

Friends, comrades and fellow South Africans.

I greet you all in the name of peace, democracy and freedom for all.

I stand here before you not as a prophet but as a humble servant of you, the people. Your tireless and heroic sacrifices have made it possible for me to be here today. I therefore place the remaining years of my life in your hands.

On this day of my release, I extend my sincere and warmest gratitude to the millions of my compatriots and those in every corner of the globe who have campaigned tirelessly for my release.

I send special greetings to the people of Cape Town, this city which has been my home for three decades. Your mass marches and other forms of struggle have served as a constant source of strength to all political prisoners.

I salute the African National Congress. It has fulfilled our every expectation in its role as leader of the great march to freedom.

I salute our President, Comrade Oliver Tambo, for leading the ANC even under the most difficult circumstances.

I salute the rank and file members of the ANC. You have sacrificed life and limb in the pursuit of the noble cause of our struggle.

I salute combatants of Umkhonto we Sizwe, like Solomon Mahlangu and Ashley Kriel who have paid the ultimate price for the freedom of all South Africans.

I salute the South African Communist Party for its sterling contribution to the struggle for democracy. You have survived 40 years of unrelenting persecution. The memory of great Communists like Moses Kotane, Yusuf Dadoo, Bram Fischer and Moses Mabhida will be cherished for generations to come.

I salute General Secretary Joe Slovo, one of our finest patriots. We are heartened by the fact that the alliance between ourselves and the Party remains as strong as it always was.

I salute the United Democratic Front, the National Education Crisis Committee, the South African Youth Congress, the Transvaal and Natal Indian Congresses and COSATU and the many other formations of the Mass Democratic Movement.

I also salute the Black Sash and the National Union of South African Students. We note with pride that you have acted as the conscience of white South Africa. Even during the darkest days in the history of our struggle you held the flag of liberty high. The large-scale mass mobilisation of the past few years is one of the key factors which led to the opening of the final chapter of our struggle.

I extend my greetings to the working class of our country. Your organised strength is the pride of our movement. You remain the most dependable force in the struggle to end exploitation and oppression.

I pay tribute to the many religious communities who carried the campaign for justice forward when the organisations for our people were silenced.

I greet the traditional leaders of our country — many of you continue to walk in the footsteps of great heroes like Hintsa and Sekhukune.

I pay tribute to the endless heroism of youth, you, the young lions. You, the young lions, have energised our entire struggle.

I pay tribute to the mothers and wives and sisters of our nation. You are the rock-hard foundation of our struggle. Apartheid has inflicted more pain on you than on anyone else.

On this occasion, we thank the world community for their great contribution to the anti-apartheid struggle. Without your support our struggle would not have reached this advanced stage. The sacrifice of the frontline states will be remembered by South Africans forever.

My salutations would be incomplete without expressing my deep appreciation for the strength given to me during my long and lonely years in prison by my beloved wife and family. I am convinced that your pain and suffering was far greater than my own.

Before I go any further I wish to make the point that I intend making only a few preliminary comments at this stage. I will make a more complete statement only after I have had the opportunity to consult with my comrades.

Today the majority of South Africans, black and white, recognise that apartheid has no future. It has to be ended by our own decisive mass action in order to build peace and security. The mass campaign of defiance and other actions of our organisation and people can only culminate in the establishment of democracy. The destruction caused by apartheid on our sub-continent is incalculable. The fabric of family life of millions of my people has been shattered. Millions are homeless and unemployed. Our economy lies in ruins and our people are embroiled in political strife. Our resort to the armed struggle in 1960 with the formation of the military wing of the ANC, Umkhonto we Sizwe, was a purely defensive action against the violence of apartheid. The factors which necessitated the armed struggle still exist today. We have no option but to continue. We express the hope that a climate conducive to a negotiated settlement will be created soon so that there may no longer be the need for the armed struggle.

I am a loyal and disciplined member of the African National Congress. I am therefore in full agreement with all of its objectives, strategies and tactics.

The need to unite the people of our country is as important a task now as it always has been. No individual leader is able to take on this enormous task on his own. It is our task as leaders to place our views before our organisation and to allow the democratic structures to decide. On the question of democratic practice, I feel duty bound to make the point that a leader of the movement is a person who has been democratically elected at a national conference. This is a principle which must be upheld without any exceptions.

Today, I wish to report to you that my talks with the government have been aimed at normalising the political situation in the country. We have not as yet begun discussing the basic demands of the struggle. I wish to stress that I myself have at no time entered into negotiations about the future of our country except to insist on a meeting between the ANC and the government.

Mr. De Klerk has gone further than any other Nationalist president in taking real steps to normalise the situation. However, there are further steps as outlined in the Harare Declaration that have to be met before negotiations on the basic demands of our people can begin. I reiterate our call for, inter alia, the immediate ending of the State of Emergency and the freeing of all, and not only some, political prisoners. Only such a normalised situation, which allows for free political activity, can allow us to consult our people in order to obtain a mandate.

The people need to be consulted on who will negotiate and on the content of such negotiations. Negotiations cannot take place above the heads or behind the backs of our people. It is our belief that the future of our country can only be determined by a body which is democratically elected on a non-racial basis. Negotiations on the dismantling of apartheid will have to address the overwhelming demand of our people for a democratic, non-racial and unitary South Africa. There must be an end to white monopoly on political power and a fundamental restructuring of our political and economic systems to ensure that the inequalities of apartheid are addressed and our society thoroughly democratised.

It must be added that Mr. De Klerk himself is a man of integrity who is acutely aware of the dangers of a public figure not honouring his undertakings. But as an organisation we base our policy and strategy on the harsh reality we are faced with. And this reality is that we are still suffering under the policy of the Nationalist government.

Our struggle has reached a decisive moment. We call on our people to seize this moment so that the process towards democracy is rapid and uninterrupted. We have waited too long for our freedom. We can no longer wait. Now is the time to intensify the struggle on all fronts. To relax our efforts now would be a mistake which generations to come will not be able to forgive. The sight of freedom looming on the horizon should encourage us to redouble our efforts.

It is only through disciplined mass action that our victory can be assured. We call on our white compatriots to join us in the shaping of a new South Africa. The freedom movement is a political home for you too. We call on the international community to continue the campaign to isolate the apartheid regime. To lift sanctions now would be to run the risk of aborting the process towards the complete eradication of apartheid.

Our march to freedom is irreversible. We must not allow fear to stand in our way. Universal suffrage on a common voters' role in a united democratic and non-racial South Africa is the only way to peace and racial harmony.

In conclusion I wish to quote my own words during my trial in 1964. They are true today as they were then:

"I have fought against white domination and I have fought against black domination. I have cherished the ideal of a democratic and free society in which all persons live together in harmony and with equal opportunities. It is an ideal which I hope to live for and to achieve. But if needs be, it is an ideal for which I am prepared to die."

Message To USA Big Business

June 19, 1990

The message we bring to you is a simple one.

It is that we look forward to the time when you will join hands with our people to form a partnership off freedom and prosperity for the peoples of South Africa and the United States of America.

We hope this meeting will begin the process of consultation among ourselves to determine what needs to be done in order to turn that partnership into a reality.

You all know that our life's work is not yet done.

We have still not attained our objective of transforming SA into a united, democratic, non-racial and non-sexist country.

Our struggle therefore continues and will continue until freedom dawns.

The kind of freedom we seek is not difficult to define.

Its fundamental principles are not different from those which you hold dear in this country.

We want to see everybody enjoying the right to vote.

The basic human rights of all our citizens have to be protected and guaranteed, to ensure the genuine liberty of every individual.

The law before which all should be equal, should rule supreme.

The racial and ethnic divisions and discriminatory practises that constitute the apartheid system have to be ended completely and without qualification.

We want to see the millions of our people build one SA Nation whose integrity will be secured by the fact of the freedom of all its members to decide their destiny, speak the language of their choice, enjoy their culture and engage in any religious practice according to their conscience.

We cannot say with any precision how soon we will bring this democratic society into being.

What however seems clear is that the road we still have to travel is immeasurably shorter than the path we had to cover to arrive at the point where we are today.

We are certain that the victory of the democratic cause is at hand.

Let me also say that none of us should seek to ignore or underestimate the fact that if today we speak of victory being in sight, as we do, it is because our people have waged a hard and long struggle to the end of the system of apartheid.

The international community has also made an important contribution to this struggle, not least through the imposition of economic and other sanctions.

We believe, and trust that you will agree with us, that since we have not yet achieved the democratic transformation we all desire, the pressure must be maintained, both internally and internationally, to bring about this result.

The processes leading to a just and lasting political settlement has started.

At the meeting we held at the beginning of last month with President De Klerk and his colleagues, it was agreed that the obstacles to negotiations that we had identified would be removed.

We believe that these will indeed be removed.

It will then be possible to take the process further on, to identify the parties to the negotiations and ultimately to draw up a new, democratic constitution and a bill of rights that would be entrenched and justiciable.

We do not, of course, underestimate the difficulties that still lie ahead of us.

We are fully conscious of the fact that our interlocutors, the ruling National Party, have up to now been a party of racism, whose reason for existence was to advance the interests of the Afrikaners specifically and the Whites in general, at the expense of the black majority.

Even now, as it talks of a non-racial democracy, this party has not yet fully abandoned the notion that the SA population should be divided into separate racial and ethnic political compartments.

It is still toying around with the idea of a white veto or a constitutional arrangement which would give the White minority exclusive power over the various elements of social activity.

In addition, there are many among our White compatriots who are opposed to democratic change, either because of outright adherence to raw and unbridled racism or because they fear democratic majority rule.

Some of these are armed.

They are to be found within both the army and the police.

Outside of these state agencies, other Whites are working frantically to liquidate the ANC, its leadership and membership, as well as other persons or formations which these right-wing terrorist group see as threat to the continued existence of the system of White minority domination.

Despite all these negatives and worrying factors, we are still of the view that change will come sooner rather than later.

The overwhelming majority of our people, including the Whites, are in favour of change.

The internal and international cost of maintaining the apartheid system has to become too high.

De Klerk and his colleagues in the leadership of the National Party have understood that they must act together with us and all other representative political forces, to bring about a new reality.

We believe that they hold this view honestly, and are ready to implement such agreements as may be arrived at democratically.

The political settlement we have been speaking of will not, however, in itself, end the massive poverty to which our people are heir.

I am certain that all of us present here will be familiar with the catastrophe of misery which is the lot of millions of our people.

I do not have to list for you the enormous needs we are faced with in terms of jobs, housing, education nutrition, health care, pensions and social security and so on.

Naturally and correctly, our people expect that the democratic state will take all necessary measures to address these issues as a matter of urgency.

The very fact that these masses will have political power in their hands will increase the pressure on the Government, at all levels, to meet these expectations.

Indeed, because the political and economic haves are White and the political and economic have-nots are black, the very stability of the political settlement depends on rapid and visible progress being made to improve the quality of life of all the people.

The private sector, both domestic and international, will have a vital contribution to make to the economic and social reconstruction of SA after apartheid.

It will be critical that the economy grows rapidly and at rates that supercede population growth.

This cannot happen without large inflows of foreign capital, including US capital.

We will also to ensure that we achieve levels of productivity which will enable us to compete on the international markets successfully.

An important requirement to enable us to achieve this, is that we must have access to the management skills, the body of technology and the risk capital which make for the success of your own corporations in both the domestic and international markets.

We are sensitive to the fact that as investors in a post-apartheid SA, you will need to be confident about the security of your investments, an adequate and equitable return on your capital and a general capital climate of peace and stability.

That is why we share the common objectives of the total abolition of the apartheid system and the institution of a genuinely democratic system in an open society.

Further to this, it is also in our interest that all investors, like our own peoples as a whole, should have confidence in the stability of the society we will seek to build.

They should know it is a matter of fact that the investment they make today, whether in the house they build, the child they educate, or the savings they put into a bank, is not likely to vanish tomorrow because of some arbitrary Government action or a social upheaval generated by continuing social injustice.

We do not have time to address other questions relating to our broad views about the future SA economy.

We believe that it will be a mixed economy, though we have no blue print as to the make-up of that mix.

The trade unions will have to enjoy the right to collective bargaining and other privileges that are normal in any democratic society.

We are convinced this economy will have to be restructured, so that it is able to serve the material interests of all our people, and not just the White minority.

Ecological issues will also have to be attended to, to ensure against, among other things, the degradation of the soil, as has happened in many parts of the country, and the pollution of the atmosphere around many black urban Townships.

We foresee the SA economy playing an important part in the regeneration and expansion of the economy of Southern Africa as a whole.

We see this regional economy, so well endowed with human and natural resources, as an outstanding growth point in the world economy.

Its good health would help to focus international opinion on the need for the rest of the world to join hands with the African continent as a whole to address the urgent needs facing the millions of people on our continent.

In summary, we count on you to take the decision that you will become part, and an important part, of the future SA economy.

To reiterate what we said at the beginning, we hope this meeting will begin the dialogue among ourselves about the system of co-operation we need to improve the lives of the people of both our countries.

Immediately, we believe that there are some other things that you should and can do.

You should continue to isolate apartheid SA.

You should reflect on what further contribution you can make to encourage the peaceful process leading to the transformation of SA into a democratic country.

You should help us with the material resources which will enable us to repatriate and resettle our compatriots whom the apartheid system forced into exile.

You should help us with the resources which will enable us to carry out the educational work among all our people which will encourage and enable them to participate in the process of negotiations.

You should help us to train significant numbers especially of black managers, both in business schools and the work place.

Together we should decide how to continue our dialogue intended to define the content and parameters of our partnership for democracy and prosperity in SA.

We trust that you will be kind enough to consider the issues we have raised, at your leisure, bearing in mind that they reflect the views of what is accepted to be one of the principal political forces in our country, without which no solution is possible.

We are very interested to discuss our common future with you, approaching all issues in a spirit of give and take, but bearing in mind that our people, as much as yours, value their freedom and independence.

But of course we also know that freedom and independence can only be exercised, and can only have true meaning, in the context of an interdependent world.

Statement At UN Special Committee Against Apartheid

June 22, 1990

Your Excellency, Ambassador Ibrahim Gamban, Permanent Representative of the Federal Republic of Nigeria and Chairman of the Special Committee against Apartheid; Your Excellency, Mr. Perez de Cuellar, Secretary-General of the United Nations; Your Excellencies, Permanent Representatives; Heads of the Observer Missions; Ladies and Gentlemen, Friends and Comrades:

We feel especially honoured and privileged to have the possibility today to stand at this particular place, to speak to all of you, who represent the peoples of the world. We are most grateful to you, Mr. Chairman, the Special Committee against Apartheid, the Secretary-General, and all the member States of this Organisation, for making it possible for us to be here.

The tragedy is that what has created the need for this gathering and made it seem natural that we must gather in this historic meeting place, is the fact of the continuing commission of a crime against humanity. How much better it would have been if we were meeting to celebrate a victory in hand, a dream fulfilled, the triumph of justice over a tyrannical past, the realisation of the vision enshrined in the UN charter and the Universal Declaration of Human Rights.

It will forever remain an indelible blight on human history that the apartheid crime ever occurred. Future generations will surely ask — what error was made that this system established itself in the wake of the adoption of a Universal Declaration on Human Rights.

It will forever remain an accusation and a challenge to all men and women of conscience that it took as long as it has, before all of us stood up to say enough is enough. Future generations will surely enquire — what error was made that this system established itself in the aftermath of the trials at Nuremburg?

These questions will arise because when this august body, the United Nations, first discussed the South African question in 1946, it was discussing the issue of racism. They will be posed because the spur to the establishment of this Organisation was the determination of all humanity never again to permit racist theory and practice to dragoon the world into the deathly clutches of war and genocide.

And yet, for all that, a racist tyranny established itself in our country. As they knew would happen, who refused to treat this matter as a quaint historical abberation, this tyranny has claimed its own conclave of victims. It has established its own brutal worth by the number of children it has killed and the orphans, the widows and widowers it can claim as its unique creation.

And still it lives on, provoking strange and monstrous debates about the means that its victims are obliged to use to rid themselves of this intolerable scourge, eliciting arguments from those who choose not to act, that to do nothing must be accepted as the very essence of civilised opposition to tyranny.

We hold it as an inviolable principle that racism must be opposed by all the means that humanity has at its disposal. Wherever it occurs, it has the potential to result in a systematic and comprehensive denial of human rights to those who are discriminated against. This is because all racism is inherently a challenge to human rights, because it denies the view that every human being is a person of equal worth with any other, because it treats entire peoples as sub-human.

This is why it was correct to characterise the apartheid system as a crime against humanity and appropriate that the international community should decide that it should be suppressed and punishment meted out against its perpetrators. We pay tribute to this Organisation and its member States for this and other decisions and actions it took to expunge this crime.

Mr. Chairman:

We also take this opportunity to salute the Special Committee against Apartheid, which has been and is a very important instrument in our struggle against the iniquitous and oppressive policies of the South African Government. We salute also the States that make up its membership who have been unrelenting in their resolve to contribute everything they could to ensure that the world was mobilised to act against the apartheid system.

In this connection also, Sir, allow us to express a well-deserved tribute to your country, Nigeria, which you so ably represent, as did your predecessor in this important office, His Excellency Major-General Joseph Garba, current President of the General Assembly, and under whose leadership the United Nations declaration on South Africa was adopted by consensus at the sixteenth special session of the General Assembly last December.

That declaration will go down in history as one of the most important documents in the struggle of the international community against apartheid. The fact that it was adopted by consensus was itself a telling blow against the apartheid system and a vital statement underlining the unity of the world community on the South African question and its resolution.

No relaxation of sanctions

We look forward to the report that the distinguished Secretary-General of the United Nations will submit dealing with the question of the implementation of the declaration in South Africa. This report will also be important to the extent that it will provide a basis for further decisions by the United Nations regarding future action on the question of apartheid.

What must however be clear is that the apartheid system remains in place. None of the principles laid down in the declaration has been implemented, to provide what the declaration characterised as an internationally acceptable solution to the South African question. Similarly, the profound and irreversible changes which the declaration visualised have not yet occurred.

The conclusion from these observations would seem clear to us. It is that nothing which has happened in South Africa calls for a revision of the positions that this Organisation has taken in its struggle against apartheid. We therefore, strongly urge that there should be no relaxation of existing measures. The sanctions that have been imposed by the United Nations and by individual governments should remain in place.

We also urge that the United Nations should do everything in its power to maintain the unity it achieved when it adopted the declaration on South Africa last December. We therefore hope that all member States will continue to act in concert so as not to create any situation in which those who are opposed to change in our country find encouragement to resist change, because some countries would have destroyed the consensus that has been achieved. In this regard, we take this opportunity once more to call on the countries of the European Community, which are holding a summit meeting in a few days, time themselves to remain faithful to the purposes of the declaration to whose elaboration they were party and for which they voted.

Present situation in South Africa

At the initiative of the ANC, the process has begun which could lead to a just political settlement in our country. At our well-known meeting in Cape Town, at the beginning of last month, we agreed with the South African Government on the removal of the obstacles to negotiations which are identified in the declaration. The process of implementing that agreement has started. But as this distinguished gathering knows, a lot still remains to be done before we can say that a climate conducive to negotiations has been created.

We therefore still have some distance to travel before we undertake the further steps outlined in the declaration, leading to negotiations for the adoption of a new, democratic constitution. The fact that a good beginning was made in Cape Town should not lead us to conclude that further progress is assured or that we will not have to confront major obstacles in future.

In this regard, we would like to reiterate what we have said before, that we believe that President de Klerk and his colleagues in the leadership of the ruling party are people of integrity. We are of the view that they will abide by decisions that are arrived at in the course of our discussions and negotiations. This, in itself, is an important victory of our common struggle because it is that struggle which has made the cost of maintaining the apartheid system too high, and helped to convince the ruling group in our country that change can no longer be resisted.

It is, however, also true that there are many among our white compatriots who are still committed to the maintenance of the evil system of white minority domination. Some are opposed because of their ideological adherence to racism. Others are resisting because they fear democratic majority rule.

Some of these are armed and are to be found within the army and the police.

Outside of these state agencies, other whites are working at a feverish pace to establish para-military groups whose stated aim is the physical liquidation of the ANC, its leadership and membership, as well as other persons or formations which these right-wing terrorist groups see as a threat to the continued existence of the system of white minority domination. We cannot afford to underestimate the threat that these defenders of a brutal and continuing reality pose to the whole process of working towards a just political settlement.

Commitment of the ANC

The ANC is determined to do everything in its power to ensure speedy movement forward towards the peaceful abolition of the apartheid system. To this end, we are engaged in many initiatives within South Africa, armed at bringing into the process of negotiations all the people and the representative political formations of our country. We have to overcome the mistrust that exists on both sides and reinforce the understanding that the only victory we should all seek is the victory of the people as a whole, and not the victory of one party over another.

It is obvious that none of these processes can be easy. We are however inspired by the experience of the people of Namibia and our comrades-in-arms of SWAPO, who also overcame the divisions and the mistrust generated by the apartheid system, carried out a peaceful political process within a relatively short period of time and are today a proud nation of independent people. We take this opportunity to salute the representatives of the Namibian people who are present in this hall and acknowledge the debt we owe them for the contribution they have made to our own liberation.

We also salute the frontline states of Southern Africa and the rest of our continent for their own enormous contribution to the struggle against apartheid, which has brought us to the point today when we can say that the victory of the struggle for a united, democratic and non-racial South Africa is within our grasp.

Tribute is also due to the non-aligned countries and movement and the peoples of the rest of the world for their own sterling efforts in pursuit of the common cause. What we must once more urge, is that all these forces should maintain their unity around the perspectives contained in the UN and Harare declarations on South Africa. How fast we progress towards liberation will depend on how successful we are in our efforts to sustain that united resolve.

This is for us a moving moment because we know that as we stand here we are among friends and people of conscience. We know this because we know what you did over the decades to secure my release and the release of other South African political prisoners from Pretoria's dungeons. We thank you most sincerely for this, especially because you have thus given us the opportunity to join hands with you in the search for a speedy solution to the enormous problems facing our country, our region and continent and humanity as a whole.

We know also that you harbour the hope that we will not relent or falter in the pursuit of that common vision which should result in the transformation of South Africa into a country of democracy, justice and peace. Standing before the nations of the world, we make that commitment, strengthened by the knowledge that you will fight on, side by side with us, until victory is achieved.

We also take this opportunity to extend warm greetings to all others who fight for their liberation and their human rights, including the peoples of Palestine and western Sahara. We commend their struggles to you, convinced that we are all moved by the fact that freedom is indivisible, convinced that the denial of the rights of one diminish the freedom of the other.

We thank you for your kind invitation to us to address this august gathering and for the opportunity it has given us to pay homage to you all, to the Secretary General, the President of the General Assembly, the Special Committee against Apartheid and the United Nations itself, for the work that has been done to end the apartheid crime against humanity.

The distance we still have to travel is not long. Let us travel it together. Let us, by our joint actions, vindicate the purposes for which this Organisation was established and where its charter and the Universal Declaration on Human Rights will become part of the body of Law on which will be based the political and social order of a new South Africa. Our common victory is assured.

Thank you.

Speech At The Rally To Relaunch The South African Communist Party

July 29, 1990

Comrade Chairman, Comrades and friends.

This is an important day in the political history of our country. It is a day which should give comfort and hope to everybody in South Africa who calls himself or herself a democrat. It is important because it marks the end of a period of exactly 40 years, during which the declared aim and practice of the state was to suppress all political opinion which was not certified by the ruling National Party as legitimate and permissible.

Surely, there are, today, happy smiles on the faces of the political thinkers who said that, though they might disagree with opposing views that some people might express, they would nevertheless defend with their lives the democratic right of such opponents to express their views.

The ANC is not a Communist Party. But as a defender of democracy, it has fought and will continue to fight for the right of the Communist Party to exist. As a movement for national liberation, the ANC has no mandate to espouse a Marxist ideology. But as a democratic movement, as a Parliament of the people of our country, the ANC has defended and will continue to defend the right of any South African to adhere to the Marxist ideology if that is their wish.

To us as a democratic movement, the lesson of our history is very clear. It is what the peoples of Europe learnt during the turbulent decade of the 1930s, when fascism began its assault on democracy by launching a violent offensive against the Communists.

It is the same lesson that the people of the United States learnt during the decade of the nineteen fifties, when the forces of McCarthyism launched an assault aimed at undermining the democratic heritage of the American people, by conducting a virulent offensive against Communist and left opinion.

Theologians of the German Church understood these processes very well when they said the Christian Church did nothing when the Nazis attacked the Communists. And again the Church did nothing when the Nazis turned their brutal attention to the Socialists. And when the Nazis turned against Christian men and women of conscience, the Church found that there was nobody to defend it.

This is a mistake the ANC never made, because we understood that the banning of the Communist Party in 1950, was but a prelude to the suppression of all democratic opinion in our country. This is a lesson that those within the National Party, who consider themselves to be democrats, need to learn very quickly.

The lesson they need to learn is that it was fundamentally wrong to have enacted the Suppression of Communism Act in 1950. The lesson they need to learn is that it is fundamentally wrong today to seek to build an atmosphere of democratic tolerance of different views by attempting to demonise those who choose to hold Communist opinions. Such a posture leads to one thing and one thing only, namely, the denial and suppression of democracy itself.

We are here today to participate with you in the public launch of the Communist Party, 40 years after it was banned. We do this because during the nearly 70 years of its existence, the Communist Party has distinguished itself as an ally in the common struggle to end the racial oppression and exploitation of the black masses of our country. It has fought side by side with the ANC for the common objective of the National Liberation of people, without seeking to impose its views on our movement.

It has been and is a dependable friend who respected our independence and our policy. Its members have been devoted Congressites who, as members of the ANC, have propagated and defended the policies of our movement, including the Freedom Charter, without hesitation. They have therefore given strength to our own movement, whatever their separate perspectives might be as an independent political formation.

Its leaders have been close friends and colleagues of the leaders of our movement. The general secretary of the Communist Party, comrade Joe Slovo, is an old friend. There is an old established friendship between his family and mine. We went to university together. We were co-accused in the Treason Trial of 1956 to 1961.

Over the years, we have shared the same views on fundamental issues to do with ending the criminal system of apartheid and the democratic transformation of our country. Today we share the same views about the vital importance and urgency of arriving at a political settlement through negotiations, in conditions of peace for all our people.

This personal and political relationship has been able to endure over the decades precisely because Joe Slovo and his colleagues in the Communist Party have understood and respected the fact that the ANC is an independent body. They have never sought to transform the ANC into a tool and a puppet of the Communist Party.

They have fought to uphold the character of the ANC as the Parliament of the oppressed, containing within it people with different ideological views, who are united by the common perspective of national emancipation represented by the Freedom Charter.

Even when we got together with comrade Joe Slovo and others in 1961 to form the People's army, Umkhonto we Sizwe, we understood the specific role that Umkhonto had to play. We understood that despite the fact that state repression had compelled us to take up arms, this did not make the ANC a slave to violence.

We knew that the cadres who made up Umkhonto we Sizwe would have to be men and women who would respect the political authority of the ANC, and always proceed from the position that they took up arms precisely to help establish a democratic order in which the people would have the right to free political opinion and expression, without fear of intimidation from any quarter.

Such are the views of the men and women in who make up our glorious army. To suggest, as some are doing these days, that these outstanding sons and daughters of our people harbour ideas of unilateral military action against the peace process, is an insult manufactured by the enemies of democracy who have built conspiratorial nests within the interstices of the power structures of this country.

Everybody, including the government, also knows that the ANC is the political formation that determines the strategic use of the weapons in the hands of the People's army. Our movement, which has a distinguished and unchallenged history of commitment to peaceful solutions, has itself never abandoned the strategy of non-violent struggle, even when the apartheid regime did everything in its power to make such struggle impossible. It cannot now turn against the peaceful resolution of the conflict in our country, precisely at the moment when such a peaceful resolution seems possible.

Those who today pose as experts on the structure and strategy of our broad movement for national liberation must understand these ABCs of our struggle. What these ABCs point to is the commitment of the alliance led by the ANC to do everything in its power to bring about a peaceful solution of the problems facing our country.

Dear comrades and friends:

The objective we have pursued since our formation 78 years ago remains unchanged. We must move with all possible speed to abolish the apartheid system and to transform South Africa into a united, democratic, non-racial and non-sexist country. We have entered into talks with the government for the realisation of these goals.

Because we have an urgent task to attain our emancipation, we insist that the talks must go on. Our freedom should not be postponed or denied simply because some people have a secret agenda to sustain an anti-democratic crusade against Communist opinion.

But we also insist that the talks must proceed in conditions of peace. Therefore the violence of the police against the people must come to an end. The violence of the black and white vigilantes against the people must come to an end. If it is genuinely interested in peace and negotiations, the government must act to bring about this result.

We wish to repeat here what the entire democratic movement of our country has said in the past — that in the context of an end to state violence against the people and a political process leading to the liquidation of the apartheid system, we ourselves are ready to discuss the suspension of our own armed actions to ensure that peace and stability prevails throughout our country.

We call on the government to respond positively to these positions, to abandon the attempt to create new obstacles by whipping up an anti-communist hysteria, to act in a responsible manner in the interests of all our people, in the interest of the cause of justice and peace.

Dear friends of the Communist Party:

We know we can count on you to stand with us as we pursue these goals. It is our profound desire that you, like all other political formations in our country, should be active participants in the historic process which should lead to the peaceful resolution of the problems confronting our country and people. We extend to you the best wishes of the People's Movement, the ANC, and look forward to continuing co-operation in the common struggle to bring freedom, peace and security to all the people of our country.

The struggle continues!

Victory is certain!

Amandla ngawethu!

Speech To The Organisation Of African Unity

September 8, 1990

As the Secretary-General of the OAU has said, we have declared a suspension of armed action with immediate effect. We have done that firstly because we are the architects of the peace process that is going on in the country today. We, the ANC, initiated this process as far back as 1986. Eventually, the government agreed to sit down and talk to us. We have had two successful meetings which raised the hope that a peaceful settlement is possible in our country. Precisely at this stage, these elements have intensified their own activities in which they are attacking the masses of the people. If the government fails to take action, I can see this process being derailed.

The danger is very great, because although we are determined to do everything to create an atmosphere whereby a peaceful settlement can be reached, we are not prepared to do so indefinitely. We are not prepared to witness the death of our people. The carrying of negotiations and rhetoric on peace while at the same time the government is conducting a war against us is a position we cannot accept. We have warned the government several times on this matter, and if they fail to take effective action the whole of South Africa, unfortunately and very much against our will, will be drowned in blood. That is the responsibility of the government. We will do everything in our power to avoid that disaster and to press on with peace.

Next stage of negotiations

The next stage in the discussions between the ANC and the government is that of identifying the people who are going to be entrusted with the task of drawing up a new constitution for the country. It must be a non-racial constitution, democratic in all aspects. In this regard, the government and the ANC take two totally different positions. According to the government, all the leaders who work through their political structures, that is, the structures which have been set up by the government over the years, must be involved in these negotiations.... They must sit around the negotiating table, and the position therefore is that the ANC and other sections of the liberation movement that might be involved in the discussions will, right from the beginning, be in the minority.

Our position is a simple one. We say: when these so-called "elected leaders" were elected, the ANC and other political organisations were banned, many of our members were driven into exile, others thrown into jails. Those that remained inside the country were banned so that the organisations themselves could not take part in those elections. If we are now going to entrust certain individuals with the task of drawing up a new non-racial constitution, these leaders must be identified through democratic and non-racial elections.

Maintain sanctions

In spite of the progressive stand of Mr. de Klerk, we are still very far from getting the fundamental and irreversible changes that we require. As I have pointed out, when I went to jail, I couldn't vote. I have come back after 27 years: I still cannot vote. That is the issue in South Africa, and until all the people of South Africa can vote and determine their own destiny there is no question whatsoever of reviewing our strategies. Sanctions and isolation of South Africa must be maintained.

The government is concerned and they are pleading to us almost daily to call upon the international community to lift sanctions. Our answer is simple: that if you want us to approach the international community to lift sanctions, we are only too ready to do that, but the price is the extension of the vote to every South African, now. That is our stand, and that is why there is an element of urgency both from the point of view of the government and the point of view of the ANC. There is a sense of urgency because we are as much concerned as the government that our economy should not be reduced to shambles. But that is the price white South Africa must pay for excluding the masses of the people from the vote and from the resources of the country.

Unity of the liberation movement

A matter which has been raised by the two previous speakers here is one of the unity of the blacks, the unity of the liberation movement. We regard this as very important, but our starting point is that in South Africa the people are united. Huge rallies that we have held since October last year have never been seen in the history of the country. We have held a number of mass actions which have had a very important impact.

We are united, but we take into account the fact that there are other political organisations whose members have sacrificed like all of us. We feel it is only fair to recognise their contributions and seek unity with them. I, as an individual, have made several efforts to see the leaders of these organisations. Some have responded very well. We are discussing with them. We have formed joint structures with them.

But there are others who have persistently taken up the attitude of refusing to sit down and talk with us. On the contrary, they are using the mass media, the white mass media, to air differences amongst us without coming to us to say: here are our differences, can we resolve them?

I appeal to them, as I have done on many occasions in South Africa, to forget the past. Let us hold hands, let us address this problem together. If we stand together, victory of the liberation movement is assured.

Statement At The World Economic Conference

February 2, 1991

Prof Klaus Shwaab, President of the World Economic Forum Distinguished Participants, Ladies and Gentlemen:

The ANC and I personally, would like to thank the World Economic Forum most sincerely for inviting us to attend and address this important gathering. We would further like to express our profound appreciation for your decision to allocate time for discussion of the South African question. We do believe that your initiative in this regard is most timely.

The impending political transformation of South Africa is part of the truly phenomenal process of renewal which our planet is experiencing. The features of this process are clear enough.

They delineate a future in which the peoples in all countries will govern themselves under open and plural democratic systems in our own country. This means the end of white minority dictatorship and the building of a new nation of many colours, languages and cultures, bound together by a common

South African patriotism, a shared spirit of nationhood and bonds of mutual dependence.

As in other parts of the world, we too will establish a society based on respect for human rights, to ensure the freedom and dignity of every individual, as an inalienable condition of human existence and development.

The new world that is being born foresees the dawn of the age of peace, in which wars within nations, between countries and among peoples will be a thing of the past.

We need to reach the point when weapons of mass destruction will themselves have been destroyed and the trade in weapons of death will have been reduced to an absolute minimum.

And yet many of these masses who are freeing themselves from tyranny and expanding the frontiers of liberty, exercising their right to self determination and committing their lives to the defence of peace and life itself, are themselves threatened by death from starvation.

The planet they inhabit faces the awesome menace of destruction as a result of a human-made ecological catastrophe.

I am certain it is a matter of common cause among us here that the continued impoverishment of millions of people throughout the world has become one of the great sources of global instability.

Those who are deprived will inevitably act to demand a better life. The gnawing pain of persistent hunger must, in the end, lead to food riots.

In response, governing authorities that will feel threatened by the rebellion of the masses will resort to repression, to a denial of political rights and a return to a world hostile to freedom; none of us want this.

The migration of people from central and south America and the Caribbean into the United States; similar movement of people from Africa, the near east and eastern Europe into western Europe; the phenomenon of boat people in the far east, all serve as safety valves helping to avert the threatening food crisis in the countries from which the emigrants originate.

But the question has to be posed and answered as to whether this is the best way to address the issue of poverty which afflicts so many countries in the world.

Is it in the long term interest of these countries and humanity as a whole, to uproot the most enterprising individuals from these communities, and dump them as unskilled and semi-skilled workers on the developed economies of the world?

Nor can the reality be ignored that in response to these population flows and to the pressure of poverty, there is, certainly in various parts of Europe, a growing tendency towards the proliferation of racist and neo-nazi ideas and the thuggery that goes with them.

I have no desire to overestimate the seriousness of this problem. But I would also like to submit that it is not one that can be ignored either, certainly those who are immediately threatened, be they black, Arab or Jew, cannot think this a matter to be treated with benign neglect.

The simple point we are trying to make is that the dire poverty of some is not an affliction which impacts only on those who are deprived. It reverberates across the globe and ineluctably impacts negatively on the whole of humanity, including those who live in conditions of comfort and plenty.

The inescapable conclusion from all this must surely be that our interdependence, bringing us together into a common global home, across the oceans and the continents, demands that we all combine to laugh a global offensive for development, prosperity and human survival.

We are aware of, and respect, the initiatives that have been undertaken in the past to address these issues, including those of the united nations, the EEC-ACP countries, the non-aligned movement, the north-south and south-south commissions, the OAU, as well as many others.

But I am certain that none of us here can assert that there does indeed exist a real and meaningful global offensive for development, prosperity and human survival, drawing into one concerted effort governments, the private sector, non-governmental organisations and the people themselves.

To come closer home and talk about the African continent. We cannot but take advantage of this occasion to reiterate the alarm that others have expressed at the continuing deterioration of conditions of life for millions of people.

There is no need for me, in front of this knowledgeable audience, to dwell at any length on the specifics of the socio-economic situation on our continent.

Suffice it to remind the conference that ten years ago already, in its report entitled "Accelerate Development in Sub-Saharan Africa: An Agenda for Action". The world bank had various things to say which should have sounded the alarm bells.

Here are two quotations from this report:

"When, in the mid-1970's, the world economy experienced inflation and recession, nowhere did the crisis hit with greater impact than in (the region of sub-Saharan Africa)."

And again:

"For most African countries, and for a majority of the African population, the record is grim and it is no exaggeration to talk of crisis. Slow overall economic growth, sluggish agricultural performance coupled with rapid rates of population increase, and balance of payments and fiscal crisis — these are dramatic indicators of economic trouble."

As can be expected, other issue are dealt with in the report, including deteriorating terms of trade, a continuous fall in exchange reserves and the Dracula of an external debt which many countries can neither avoid nor afford.

With regard to the current situation, the secretary general of the united nations reported only last year that in the period up to 1990, "The average African continued to get poorer and to suffer a persistent fall in an already meagre standard of living".

In his report on the "UN Programme of Action for African Economic Recovery and Development", the Secretary General speaks of the African continent sinking deeper into "an unrelenting crisis of tragic proportions".

He goes on to say that "overcoming this crisis represents the greatest development challenge of our time."

Therefore, perhaps more than any other part of the world, the situation in sub-Saharan Africa, which has worsened since the World Bank report we have cited was published, illustrates the importance of the global offensive for development, prosperity and human survival for which we have called.

Quite clearly, for this project to record success, it would be necessary that a massive transfer of resources takes place from north to south. Let me hasten to state it here that we are by no means suggesting that this is an easy objective to achieve.

Nor are we suggesting that the issue be approached either as an act of charity or as an attempt to improve the lived of the have-nots by impoverishing the haves. Rather we are suggesting that it is necessary that these transfers take place as a necessary condition to achieved development, prosperity and survival for humanity as a whole.

We say this fully aware of the general shortage of capital in the world, its sensitivity to economic imperatives and its mobility.

We also say this knowing that the underdeveloped countries themselves have to continue addressing such issues as better utilisation of resources and management of their economies, better governance, human resource development, including the upliftment and liberation of women, as well as the protection of the environment.

Among other things that the concerted global offensive would have to deal with are, of course, the debt problem, the issue of the continuous decline in the prices of commodities that the poorer countries export and access to markets for their manufactured goods.

We would like to take advantage of this opportunity to bring to your attention, as others have done before, the problems that many African and other poor countries experience as they implement structural adjustment programmes. Carried out without providing a social net to cushion their impact on those who are already gravely disadvantaged, these programmes may create more problems than they solve.

Naturally, we must also express our own unease at any developments which might result in investor attention being directed exclusively at central and eastern Europe, to the exclusion of Africa and the rest of the third world.

Nor would it be beneficial to allow the positive processes leading to European integration to result in a "fortress Europe" and, *inter alia*, the delinkage of Africa from this and other areas of the world.

My own country, South Africa, is marching on its own road to liberation and democracy. The specific process in which we are engaged, epitomised by the convention for a democratic South Africa, may not themselves be irreversible.

Nevertheless, it is quite clear that there is no force that can permanently stop our advance towards the transformation of South Africa into a united, democratic, non-racial and non-sexist country.

We want to see established, as quickly as possible, a multi-party democracy, enshrined in a constitution which provides for one person one vote on a common voters roll, separation of powers between the legislature, executive and judiciary, and devolution of power to regional and local levels of government, furthermore, we would also like to see an entrenched bill of rights, protected by an independent and representative judiciary.

Equally protected should be the rights of all our people to language, culture and religion. Further than this, we have said in the past that we are willing to look at any proposals aimed at addressing the fears of any of our population groups, provided that this was not in furtherance of apartheid and intended to subvert the normal democratic practice of majority rule.

We need to make the point also that we are against the notion of a prolonged transitional period, we have therefore put forward the suggestion that this period, beginning with the establishment of an interim or transitional government around the middle of this year, should not last longer than months.

Thus, we are determined to end apartheid and liberate ourselves as a matter of urgency. We are as equally determined that this transformation should bring with it real changes in the material conditions of life of the people.

This is dictated both by the fact of the widespread and endemic poverty that affects millions of black people in our country and the need to guarantee the success and permanence of democratic change.

This will require that all necessary measures are taken to ensure the growth of the South African economy, pulling it out of the recession and decline in which it is now enmeshed.

This will require a rapid and sustained growth in terms of capital formation or fixed investment, drawing on both domestic and external sources to finance this investment. It will also require a rapid and sustained expansion of the domestic market, as well as improved access to international markets.

Inevitably, we must address the critical question of achieving high levels of productivity for both capital and labour. At the same time, we must attend to the issue of equitable distribution of income and wealth, without which the domestic market will remain small and social stability impossible to achieve.

We visualise a mixed economy, in which the private sector would play a central and critical role to ensure the creation of wealth and jobs. Side by side with this, there will be a public sector perhaps no different from such countries as Germany, France and Italy where public enterprises constitute 9, 11 and 15 per cent of the economy respectively, and in which the state plays an important role in such areas as education, health and welfare.

For it to succeed, to achieve such basic objectives as creating wealth and jobs, ending poverty and creating a just and equitable society, future economic policy will also have to address such questions as security of investments and the right to repatriate earnings, realistic exchange rates, the rate of inflation and the fiscus.

We firmly believe that the South African economy has the potential for a very bright and exciting future. It is in our interest that this economy should thrive as never before. We are equally convinced that it will also offer very good prospects for the investors present in this room, both South African and international.

We therefore urge you to enter into a partnership with the people of South Africa, who would like to act together with you to rebuild their country to the mutual benefit. We invite you to begin now to investigate the business possibilities in our country so that you are able to move with all due speed when the moment is opportune.

In this regard, we should once more explain that our own considered position is that remaining economic sanctions should be lifted once an interim government has been established. Furthermore, we are determined to move forward as speedily as possible to establish the political and social climate which is necessary to ensure business confidence and create the possibility for investors to make long term commitments to help develop the South African economy.

South Africa is also part of a region of the world which has a population of anything up to 150 million people. This region must and will grow and develop in an integrated manner and will thus provide a sizeable market for those investors who take advantage of the opportunities this region offers and bring in the resources necessary for its development.

We must also make the point that current developments in various parts of this region point to a common striving to reinforce the democratic process, entrench a human rights culture, end civil wars and the creation of large refugee populations.

It also seems inevitable that sooner or later the peoples of the region will also begin discussing such issues as regional economic cooperation and integration, a regional security system based, inter alia, on the reduction of armed forces and military expenditures as well as coordinated measures for the protection of the environment.

In brief, we strongly believe that the region of southern Africa as a whole offers the possibility for us all to implement the perspired of the global offensive for development, prosperity and human survival of which we have spoken.

Needless to say, success in this great and historic venture would do wonderful things to address the concern which is common to all of us, of achieving the regeneration of African societies and the upliftment of its peoples.

Let me end with a special appeal to you all, who constitute a critical component part of the leadership of the peoples of the world.

If the voices of millions have been freed to enunciate the political aspirations of the people, those voices will also surely speak loudly, proclaiming an urgent desire for an end to poverty and for a more equitable distribution of opportunities, income and wealth within and among the nations.

We believe that those voices must be listened to and the concerns they express addressed. If the political transformations taking place across the globe are anything to go by, it would seem clear that these masses will not allow themselves to be silenced.

They will not be fobbed off with polite and courteous but meaningless responses. Nor will they accept the promise of jam tomorrow if they see nothing being done today to deliver the promised jam.

Motivated by nothing other than the fact of our common humanity and informed by the realisation of the common destiny of the peoples of all continents, let us then do together what we can and must do together in the interests of all humanity, while each one of us also does what he or she must do in pursuit of their enlightened self-interest but recognising, in the end, that no man is an island.

Ceremony for the Award of the Felix Houphouet-Boigny Peace Prize

February 3, 1992

Mr. Master of Ceremonies, Mr. Director-General of UNESCO, Your Excellencies, Members of the Diplomatic Corps, Distinguished Guests, Ladies and Gentlemen,

Firstly, permit me to express my profound and heartfelt appreciation of this honour that the Jury of the Felix Houphouet-Boigny Foundation for Peace Research has deemed fit to bestow on me. I accept this esteemed prize in all humility and in full knowledge that it is not the individual, Nelson Mandela, who is being so honoured, but rather the struggle for freedom and democracy in South Africa, with which my life has been so intertwined.

It is a hopeful sign of the potential of my country that this year this prize is shared by two people who trace their respective political ideals to opposing poles on our national political spectrum. It is the hope of all South Africans that this joint award signifies the convergence of our aims and a growing consensus that has begun to emerge amongst the overwhelming majority of South Africans about the future direction of our country. That developing national mood finds expression in the Convention for a Democratic South Africa which has placed before all of us the imperative that collectively commence the task of building a non-racial democracy.

It has been no easy assignment to build that consensus. Our country has finally arrived at it by a route that was extremely painful and which entailed great costs amongst which we must count human lives lost and broken. Perhaps history will one day record and enumerate the many lost opportunities.

South Africa is distinguished as a country to which history bequeathed two divergent nationalisms. These two, African and Afrikaner nationalism, embody fundamentally different perspectives on the character and the future of our country.

Because both nationalisms lay claim to the same piece of earth, our common home South Africa, the contest between them was bound to be both heated and brutal.

We are confident that the progress we are making in the CODESA talks will lay the basis for an end at least to the more violent aspects of that contest.

The shared commitment to democracy of all the participants in the Convention for a Democratic South Africa is indicative of a considerable narrowing of the distance that formerly separated Black from White in our country. It requires courage and vision on the part of all our political leaders to grasp the challenge presented by this unique moment. Posterity will not forgive us if we let slip this opportunity to move as painlessly as possible towards the goal of a country that is free and at peace with itself and its neighbours.

Eighty years ago, when the founders of the African National Congress gathered in the city of Bloemfontein, our movement embraced certain universally accepted core principles that form the basis of modern human rights culture. We have waged struggle and nursed the tender shoots of this culture in our country against great odds.

Reduced to their essentials these principles are that:

governments must derive their authority from the consent of the governed;

no person or group of persons should be subjected to oppression, domination or discrimination by virtue of his/her race, gender, colour or religious belief;

all persons should enjoy security in their persons and their goods against intrusions by secular or clerical authorities;

all persons shall enjoy the right to life, unfettered by impositions from either the secular or clerical authorities;

all persons should have the untrammelled right to hold and express whatever opinions they wish to subscribe to as long as the exercise of that right does not infringe on the rights of others.

In accepting this prize today we feel that the Jury is acknowledging the abiding value of these principles and endorses them as sound.

The past 12 months have witnessed many earth-shaking developments in various parts of the world. The march to greater democracy has not left the African continent behind. In every part of our continent the search for greater democracy and to inject real meaning into freedom and democracy is proceeding apace. We wish to associate ourselves and our movement with this great tide of freedom in the conviction that responsible government is a function not of wise rulers but rather of a people who are politically engaged.

The commitment of ANC to these values derives from our understanding of their essential purpose, that is the empowerment of the individual citizen, irrespective of his/her status, by equipping him/her to cope with the complexities of life. South Africa cries out for peace and for democracy. It is our considered judgment that we shall not have the one without the other. What we seek to build in South Africa is a society centred on human needs and aspirations. This requires that we eschew the misanthropic ideology of racism and apartheid. We as South Africans must part company with policies that render human beings the objects of manipulation by political and economic powers for the benefit of a privileged few. Our country must develop a national commitment to create conditions that shall enhance the dignity of all those living within it.

The oppressed majority in South Africa have waged struggle to capture for themselves the right to determine their own destiny, including the right to determine for themselves what to do with their future. The indispensable condition for that is the achievement of democracy. We consider that a goal that is worthy of the support of the entire international community. This prize to us has meaning because it symbolizes that support.

Thank you.

Democracy — The Only Solution

July 1, 1992

It is said that South Africa's progress has been based on "economic windfalls and political disasters". The political disasters continue. The economic windfalls have been supplanted by a wholly mismanaged economy.

Unemployment is running as high as 40 per cent! Millions of Rands of taxpayers' money, supposedly earmarked for black advancement, are embezzled by government officials with impunity. The social fabric of our country is being torn to shreds by the violence sweeping through the black townships. The NP Government, its surrogates, the state security forces and the police have been, and continue to be, directly and indirectly involved in this violence.

Such is the havoc created by the NP Government. Unless we immediately find a way out, it will cast a long shadow over future generations.

When the Government of F.W. de Klerk yielded to pressure for a negotiated solution which would bring out a united, democratic, non-racial and non-sexist South Africa, there were expectations that this process would soon realise a stable basis for addressing the numerous problems of our country.

Two and a half years down this road we are at an impasse. The essence of the problem is that the ruling minority Government continues to look for ways and means by which it can guarantee itself continued exercise of power regardless of the support by which it can muster in democratic elections.

The notion of "power sharing" which the NP of F.W. de Klerk is putting forward is that the political majority, no matter how large, should be subjected to veto by the political minority. Periodic and regular multiparty elections, the party of F.W. de Klerk is rejecting under the guise of seeking a so-called "power sharing" arrangement.

That is why they insisted at CODESA that the Constituent Assembly should take decisions by an extraordinary high majority of 75%. That is why they still adamantly insist that the new constitution should not be a constitution enacted by an elected Constituent Assembly. That is why they insist on the decisions of the Constituent Assembly being subject to veto by a second house. And that is why they wanted regional powers, duties and functions to be pre-determined at CODESA so that the sovereign power of the Constituent Assembly shall have been eroded.

And yet on all previous occasions when whites amongst themselves adopted South African Constitutions by Referendum, the National Party has always maintained that a simple majority of 50 per cent plus one suffices.

Our position is that the Constituent Assembly should take decisions by a two thirds majority, as happened in Namibia. This would ensure that the new constitution has a broad enough base of support to lay the foundations of a stable democratic society in the future.

We cannot accept an undemocratic constitution in order to address the fears of a minority party about its own future at the cost of democracy itself. As long as the Government of F.W. de

Klerk insists on a minority veto, in whatever form, the negotiations deadlock will remain.

The longer this outcome is delayed the more difficult it will be to reach an agreement and the more difficult it will be to govern in the future.

It is this stubbornness of the NP government in clinging to a minority veto that makes it inevitable that the voteless majority have to pursue genuine negotiations, side by side with exerting maximum internal and external pressure, particularly through a mass movement for democracy, peace and justice.

For as long as our people are denied the democratic vote, they shall have to vote with their feet.

It serves no purpose that the NP government whip itself into a frenzy trying to blame violence on the mass campaign for democracy conducted by the ANC and its allies. We have always sought solutions that will reduce conflict and defuse tension.

It was only through all-round internal and external pressure that the NP government was forced to acknowledge the need for a negotiated solution. If negotiations are to have any prospect of success, such pressure is now more than ever necessary.

There is indeed an explosive situation prevailing in our country. The reason for this lies in government intransigence and in it's involvement by omission and commission in the violence.

Discipline has always been the hallmark of our campaigns. Commentators are unanimous. The Peoples's Assemblies held on the 2nd February, 1992 were peaceful and disciplined. So too were the more than 70 rallies held throughout the country on June the 16th. This is the tradition in which we have mobilised our people to exercise an inherent right no authoritarian rule can take away from us.

All the efforts of the ANC and all the energies of our people are being mobilised today to force the Government away from the perilous path it is following. Now, more than ever, all South Africans, black and white together, need to join hands for democracy, peace and justice. We can ensure that elections for a democratic Constituent Assembly take place before the end of this year. Indeed, we have to make sure that it happens. Time has run out.

Statement At The United Nations Security Council

July 15, 1992

Mr. President, Distinguished Members of the Security Council, Your Excellency, Dr Boutrous Boutrous Ghali, Secretary General of the United Nations, Ministers and Ambassadors, Ladies and Gentlemen,

First of all, we would like to express our appreciation to the Security Council for agreeing to convene on the question of South Africa. We would also like to thank you most sincerely for giving us the opportunity to address you.

The United Nations has been seized with the question of South Africa for the past 45 years.

The reason for this is that our people have been subjected to the policy of apartheid, which the United Nations has determined is a crime against humanity, and helping to transform our country into a non-racial democracy. This objective has not yet been achieved.

South Africa continues to be governed by a white minority regime. The overwhelming majority of our people are still denied the vote. They remain deprived of the right to determine their destiny.

Representatives of the South African government will also address you today. However sweet-sounding the words they may utter, they represent the system of white minority rule to which the United Nations is opposed. They continue to govern our country under a constitution which the Security Council has declared null and void.

Precisely because its purposes have not yet been achieved, the United Nations must remain seized with the question of South Africa. It must continue to look for ways and means by which it can help to expedite the process leading to the democratic transformation of our country.

In the meantime an extremely critical situation has arisen.

Whereas in the Declaration of Intent adopted at the Convention for a Democratic South Africa on the 21st December, 1991 we all committed ourselves to set in motion the process whereby a democratic constitution would be drafted and adopted for a united, non-racial and non-sexist South Africa, the process is deadlocked.

The problem is that the ruling white minority government continues to look for ways and means by which it can guarantee itself the continued exercise of power, regardless of its electoral support. The regime insists that the political majority, no matter how large, should be subjected to veto by minority political parties. Unless government is forthcoming with a firm commitment to full democracy based on internationally accepted principles, and an acceptance of a sovereign and democratic constitution-making body, the process will not move forward.

But the Council meets today because this process has been brought to a halt by the carnage in the black townships. Over the last five to six years, at least 11,000 people have died as a result of this violence. During the month of June 1992 there have been 373 deaths and 395 injuries. 1,806 have been killed and 2,931 injured during the period January 1992 to June 1992.

Control of state power by the National Party regime allows it the space to deny and cover up the role of the regime, its surrogates, the state security forces and the police in fostering and fomenting the violence. Our Memorandum of the 9th July, 1992 to Mr. F. W. De Klerk sets out the evidence of numerous instances, both of acts of omission and commission, which bear out government involvement in the violence. In particular, we draw your attention to the annexure entitled "Involvement of the Security Forces in the fomenting and escalation of violence", and Annexure 3 entitled "South African Government Support for the Inkatha Freedom Party".

Mr. President:

Many years of struggle both inside and outside of South Africa brought us to the point in 1989 when, in its consensus Declaration on Apartheid and its Destructive Consequences in Southern Africa, the General Assembly concluded that circumstances existed for a negotiated resolution of the South Africa question.

In that Declaration the General Assembly said that such negotiations should, as a result of agreements that would be entered into by the liberation movement and the government, be conducted in an atmosphere free of violence.

We were and are in full agreement with these positions. They were adopted by the General Assembly precisely because it was correctly foreseen that the process of negotiations could not succeed while a virtual civil war raged in the country.

Pursuant to this objective, in August 1990 the ANC decided to suspend all armed actions. We did this unilaterally as a demonstration of our good faith and to help create an atmosphere free of violence.

At the same time it was expected that, for its part, the regime would carry out various measures which would remove obstacles to negotiations, and that it would ensure that a proper climate for negotiations did in fact exist.

Instead we have been confronted with an escalating spiral of violence.

An independent socio-political and development agency known as Community Agency for Social Enquiry (CASE) has prepared five reports with regard to the pattern of violence. One of these reports comes to the conclusion that:

"The violence appears to be switched on and off at strategic moments."

It continues:

"Behind the scale of brutality ... is the clear evidence that the violence erupts at points when it most weakens the ANC and its Allies and dies down dramatically when it would most harm the government of F. W. De Klerk."

It then goes on to say:

"Two political parties have clearly benefited from the Reef violence. The first is the National Party government... The second major beneficiary has been Inkatha."

Another report deals with 13 attacks on funerals or funeral vigils which took place on the Reef between July, 1990 and July, 1991. This study concludes that there is "an overwhelming predominance of acts of aggression carried out by supporters of the Inkatha Freedom Party. Those attacks, moreover, are carried out with the active or passive support of the South African Police".

It is more than clear to us that this violence is both organised and orchestrated. It is specifically directed at the democratic movement, whose activists, members and supporters make up the overwhelming majority of its victims.

It constitutes a cold blooded strategy of state terrorism intended to create the conditions under which the forces responsible for the introduction and entrenchment of the system of apartheid would have the possibility of imposing their will on a weakened democratic movement at the negotiations table.

However, as had been foreseen by this Organisation, this violence also has the effect of making negotiations impossible. Already in April 1991, when this campaign of terror grew to new heights, we were left with no choice but to suspend the bilateral negotiations with the regime until it took various measures to address the question of violence.

It is now common cause that the agreements that the government reached with the ANC in May 1991 aimed at curbing the violence have not been carried out by the regime.

Faced with the horrendous escalation of the violence, as evidenced in the Boipatong Massacre, occurring in the context of the negotiations deadlock, the ANC has been forced to withdraw from the multilateral process of negotiations which had been taking place in the Convention for a Democratic South Africa.

The blame for this lies squarely at the door of the regime. It, and nobody else, has the law enforcement personnel and the legal authority to stop this violence and to act against the perpetrators.

As the governing authority, it has the obligation to protect the lives and property of all the people. It has failed dismally to do this.

The regime's actions, including its persistent efforts to shift the blame for the violence and the responsibility to act against it to political organisations, have served to ensure the escalation of the carnage.

Though the causes of the violence are many and complex, it is important that we should all have a clear perspective. It is the regime which controls state power with the capacity to bring the violence to an end. Complicity of state security forces is established by the evidence which emerged in numerous court trials, inquests and commissions and is recognised in the

Goldstone Commission as well as reports of international fact finding missions.

It is also clear that the central thrust of the violence is to weaken the ANC and the democratic movement of the country.

In the face of this situation, it is also true that there are instances of counter violence by members of the democratic movement. At the same time, it is a matter of public record that the ANC policy stands opposed to the promotion of violence. We remain firmly committed to this position. But our task of ensuring that this policy position is fully and completely adhered to is made more than difficult because of the practice of the state security forces, its surrogates and the fact that it is the police controlled by the regime who remain in charge of investigating the violence, in which the state security forces are implicated, and bringing the perpetrators to book.

The ANC maintains that government culpability for the violence extends to acts of commission as well as omission.

The International Commission of Jurists, and Amnesty International, have blamed the government for failure to act against the violence. Amnesty International notes the government's "failure to bring to justice all but a tiny proportion of those involved in human rights violations ..."

Judge Goldstone in his report dated the 6th July, 1992, complains of several instances where the authorities have ignored the recommendations of his Commission.

Not a single person has been convicted in connection with the 49 massacres that claimed the lives of at least ten people in each of the incidents that have occurred in the past two years.

Where there have been proper investigations and vigorous prosecution as resulted from the Trust Feed Massacre of December 1988, convictions have been secured. Those convicted were policemen.

In 1985 Matthew Goniwe and three other Eastern Cape leaders were murdered. In May this year a document, whose authenticity has not been challenged, a message from the SADF military intelligence chief, General C. P Van der Westhuizen (then a Brigadier) proposed to the State Security Council that the four authorise "the urgent removal from society" of Goniwe and the others. No move has been made to suspend Van der Westhuizen from his position.

No action has been taken to suspend the head of the SAP forensic laboratories, General Lothar Neethling, after a Supreme Court civil case finding in January 1991 that his involvement in the poisoning of activists was on the balance of probabilities true.

Despite a judicial commission finding, implicating several Civil Cooperation Bureau (CCB) members in political violence, none has been charged. At least 20 CCB members, and probably many more, remain on the SADF payroll. Others have been offered or received huge pensions. Several have demanded immunity from prosecution.

In February 1992 it came to light that local white policemen based at the Ermelo police station encouraged and actively helped a gang of vigilantes in Wesselton. No policemen concerned has been suspended.

In an official operation in 1986 the SADF gave military training in Namibia to 200 Inkatha members who were later absorbed into the KwaZulu Police. Several trainees, in sworn affidavits, claimed to have been trained in offensive warfare. The regime has dismissed this incident on the grounds that they received VIP protection training. Some of the trainees have subsequently been implicated in the violence in Natal.

No action has been taken to control and limit the powers of the KwaZulu Police. Extensive evidence exists of KwaZulu partiality and involvement in the violence in the Natal province.

However, as recently as July 1st, 1992 the powers of the KZP have in fact been strengthened. From that date the South African Police's Internal Stability Unit will only act on unrest in

KwaZulu if called on to do so by the KZP District Commissioner.

In 1990 the Pretoria regime issued specific proclamations legalising the carrying of dangerous weapons in public. This repealed a prohibition which had been in force sine 1891.

In other words, after the ANC and other organisations were unbanned in 1990, the Pretoria regime has created a situation in which hordes of men would spill out into the streets and enter public places with the most dangerous weapons. The government is unable to explain why it virtually gave people the license to kill and maim. It has never explained why its police and army regularly accompanied these killers after many murderous rampages and arrested nobody.

We charge, without equivocation, that there is a rational basis for these acts of omission on the part of the South African government. The hard facts of the matter are the South African government has never relented in its war against the democratic movement in our country.

Recently a covert police unit, operating in the area around Boipatong, came to public attention. It, and ten others operating in other regions of the country, exist for the purpose of suppressing the democratic movement which the government still regards as the enemy and a threat to so-called national security. Former officers and personnel of the Security Police have been redeployed into these clandestine networks.

There are persistent allegations that members of these units as well as those in Special Force units composed of foreign nationals, such as Angolans, Mozambicans and Namibians, are engaged in covert operations that include the assassination of leaders and activists of the democratic movement. They are also implicated in carrying out acts of terror against the population at large.

In order to confuse the issue and evade its responsibilities the government insists that the source of the violence is rivalry between the ANC and the Inkatha Freedom Party. The fact of the matter however is that the IFP has permitted itself to become an extension of the Pretoria regime, its instrument and surrogate.

Its activities have been financed by the South African government. Its members have been armed and trained by the South African government. There is an abundance of evidence that it continues to benefit from covert co-operation with the South African government.

It therefore becomes unclear whether its members act as an independent force or as an agency on behalf of the South African government. However, it is not an independent force with whom the ANC must enter into an agreement to end the violence as the Pretoria regime asserts.

The documentation we have given to members of the Council details all the points we have raised, all of which confirm the criminal failure of the government properly to address the question of political violence which has claimed too many lives already, is tearing our country apart, and making the process of negotiations impossible.

We would like to recall earlier decisions of this Council to help the people of South Africa to transform their country into a non-racial democracy. We believe that commitment places an urgent obligation on the Council to intervene in the South African situation to end the carnage.

The very interest of the Council to see the negotiations resumed so that a peaceful solution can be found, in keeping with the democratic principles contained in the General Assembly Declaration on Southern Africa of 1989 and the resolutions of the Security Council, itself requires of the Council that it act on this matter of violence in South Africa firmly and with the necessary speed.

We believe that this violence, like the system of apartheid itself, is a direct challenge to the authority of the Council and a subversion of its global tasks of furthering peace and promoting the objectives contained in both the UN Charter and the Declaration on Human Rights.

Failure on the part of the Council to act firmly and decisively cannot but undermine its prestige and authority at a time when the Council and the United Nations as a whole are called upon to play an even more active role in the ordering of world affairs.

We would therefore urge that the Council should request the Secretary General to appoint a special representative on South Africa.

This representative should move speedily to investigate the situation in South Africa with a view to helping the Council to decide on the measures it should take to help us end the violence. The Council should then take the necessary decisions to implement such measures, including the continuous monitoring of the situation, to ensure the effectiveness of such measures as it would have undertaken.

We would also like to bring it to the notice of the Council, for the purpose of its information, that we have required of the government that it also completes the process of the release of political prisoners as well as the repeal of repressive legislation.

Again these are concrete steps visualised in the UN Declaration to create a climate conducive to negotiations. That these matters remain on the agenda more than two years after we entered into a formal agreement with the South African government that they would be attended to, demonstrates the problem we face of the reliability of the government in terms of implementing agreements it has entered into.

We would also like to take advantage of this opportunity to reaffirm our own commitment both to the process of negotiations and to a genuinely democratic outcome.

In this regard, we would again like to inform you that we have still to convince the government that it also should be committed to such a democratic outcome, accepting such ordinary concepts of a democratic system as majority rule and the absence of vetoes by minority parties.

We therefore still need to overcome these obstacles so that the process of negotiations itself, as conducted within the Convention for a Democratic South Africa, can succeed.

We would further like to assure the Council that we, who are after all the victims of the evil system of apartheid, are determined that the process of negotiations should lead to a democratic outcome as soon as possible.

We therefore need no urging regarding this matter. What we do need is the assistance of this august body to help us reopen the door to bona fide negotiations.

Mr. President, Distinguished Members of the Council,

We thank you for the opportunity you have given us to address the Council and hope that you will respond to our appeal to help us end the carnage in South Africa with the understanding of the gravity of the situation which we know you share. Our people look forward to your decisions with great expectation.

Thank you.

Press Statement, ANC/NP Summit Meeting

September 26, 1992

This summit has taken place at a time when our country is being systematically torn apart by violence. Many have died and continue to die. Free political activity does not exist in many parts of South Africa.

Our people and the world in general looked to this summit with the hope that we have begun today to rescue our people from this chaos. They looked to this summit today with the fervent wish that we can resume the process of negotiation that will take us forward to our final goal of democracy for all South Africans.

In answer to these hopes and expectations, I believe we can say that we have succeeded.

The major concerns addressed at today's summit were the release of political prisoners, steps to curtail violence emanating from hostels, and the prohibition of the carrying and display of dangerous weapons.

On the question of political prisoners, this summit today confirmed agreement reached in the past few days. We are happy and indeed jubilant to welcome the 150 of our comrades released today and look forward to the release of all remaining political prisoners by 15 November 1992. We look forward to the release on Monday 28 September of comrades Nondula, Mncube, McBride and Mjingwana.

Significant progress was also reached today with regard to hostels and dangerous weapons. Practical implementation has been agreed upon to ensure that a proclamation will be issued to prohibit the carrying and display of dangerous weapons at all public occasions subject to exemptions based upon guidelines being prepared by the Goldstone Commission. The granting of exemptions shall be entrusted to one or more retired judges designated in each province who if necessary, may be assisted by independent assessors.

On the issue of hostels, the government undertook, amongst other things, to fence identified hostels by 15 November 1992. Interim measures will also be immediately undertaken should there be any delay in this process. The continued denial of free political activity in some bantustans remains a major obstacle and must be addressed.

The government expressed its concern about our current programme of mass action. The ANC appreciates these concerns. In view of the progress made in this summit and in view of the further progress likely to be made when negotiations resume, the ANC delegation have undertaken in consultation with our structures and constituency, to examine this programme as a matter of urgency.

Finally, with regard to the constitutional process which was aborted in June this year, common understanding has been reached today in the joint Record of Understanding that we need to move with all urgency towards an interim government of national unity and a democratically elected constituent assembly. It is only the achievement of these goals that will finally bring lasting peace to this blood-soaked land. The points of agreement outlined in the Record of Understanding constitute an important step forward toward breaking the Codesa 2 deadlock.

There is obviously still much work to be done to complete this process. To this end, the summit agreed that we and the government need to engage in intensive bilaterals, a *lekgotla*, to resolve outstanding issues. We will accordingly recommend this to our National Executive Committee.

It is the duty now of all South Africans to ensure that our efforts today and the sacrifices of so many are not in vain. Let us move forward with courage, honesty and determination to build upon and consolidate the basis laid at today's summit to create a peaceful, just and democratic South Africa.

There is no reason why a political settlement should not be achieved within a relatively short period. This will pave the path to peace. This will pave the path to the economic recovery we all yearn for. But we will only achieve this if all parties and all our people, black and white, put South Africa first.

Speech To The National Conference On AIDS

October 23, 1992

Comrades and Compatriots

When I was asked to open this conference some months ago, I felt greatly honoured by the invitation and at the same time, greatly humbled by the enormity of this problem facing our own country and many other countries. My mind was sharply focused on the words in Hemingway's novel that: "man is not an island, he is not an entity unto himself, therefore ask not for whom the bells toll, they toll for thee".

The reality of the AIDS epidemic worldwide is that it is not merely a medical condition, it is a disease with socio-medical implication.

In South Africa, this problem challenges the entire socio-economic fabric of our society and poses a threat to future generations. Statistics indicate that those forced to live in poor socio-economic conditions are the highest at risk in our population.

As at the 30th June this year, 1316 cases of AIDS were recorded, and to majority of these were recorded in Natal, with the highest incidences of AIDS countrywide being recorded in the urban areas. Apartheid's legacy has played a great role in this factor, particularly in the black communities where overcrowding in homes does not provide for privacy within the family; where lack of housing and the creation of informal settlements as well as the lack of recreation facilities makes the black community even more susceptible to the sex related virus.

Single sex hostels lead to the disintegration of family units in rural areas and hostel dwellers are forced to have casual relationships since they cannot live with their families.

Another startling statistic is the incidence of AIDS in young children. Most children born with the AIDS virus, die before they reach their second birthday. The fact that the virus attacks the most economically active age group in our population, is also an issue worthy of discussion.

The serious consequences of inadequate health care facilities nationally. As well as the fact that there is limited access to the health facilities which treat sexually transmitted diseases, is a matter which this conference must pay serious attention to.

Women are the most seriously affected by the AIDS virus. They are the poorest people in our country due to the lack of education and work opportunities. The position of women in our society forces them into a situation where they are unable to protect themselves or an unborn infant against the virus. Many women find it very difficult to insist that their partners wear condoms due to the socialisation of both men and women on the issue of sex.

Our most potent weapon against this virus is education. We have, perhaps, for some time, allowed ourselves to believe that like other epidemics it will come and go; that the great advances of our time in science and technology will offer us appropriate quick intervention.

The key to our success is our own collective effort. The time for rhetorical arguments and victim blaming has passed. Now is the time for action. What we know about this disease already is enough to enable us to put in place comprehensive and appropriate intervention strategies.

We already know that AIDS has no cure and no vaccine despite the intensive research efforts. Therefore, prevention remains for us the strategy we must employ.

We do have a problem with the efforts being made by the South African government, in that the efforts by the government to introduce preventative measures are viewed with suspicion and as a ploy to control the population. This government does not have the credibility to convince the majority of black South Africans to change their sexual behaviour.

Our first thought must be the protection of our people against this disease, and therefore, it is necessary that we adopt a broad front approach to the problem.

All sectors of our community must become engaged in this battle and resources available from the government must be distributed to our communities. This problem does not allow anyone the luxury of political bias or hearts-and-minds-winning exercises. We need to set up a structure at national, regional and local level which goes beyond health workers and the government.

AIDS exposes an aspect of our lives that we are most loath to discuss openly, but it also touches on religious and cultural sensitivities. We must be sensitive to these, yet be bold to explore all avenues that will ensure that our message is not only received but well received. The only sure way of achieving this is by involving all of us in our home, our institutions, organisations, places of worship and work.

I believe that a central component of our intervention strategy must be to strengthen the capacity of our people individually and collectively to recognise, understand and act decisively against this scourge.

Let us ensure that everybody understand that a successful fight against AIDS, is not a success only for individuals, but for families, communities and indeed for our country as a whole.

In this regard I wish to make a special appeal to the government, the business community and other formations to, as a matter of urgency, make resources available for a speedy implementation of the recommendations that will come from this convention. I have already said that education is our most potent medicine against this virus—we need to bring home to parents, church leaders, political organisations and all other organs of civil society that stigmatisation of AIDS victims does not solve the problem. The victims of AIDS are victims of the illnesses in our society and we need to proceed from that basis.

Many of us find it difficult to talk about sex to our children, but nature's truth is that unless we guide the youth towards safer sex, the alternative is playing into the hands of a killer disease. In this regard I wish to endorse the idea of an AIDS charter which will educate and activate our population, as well entrench the rights of AIDS victims. Compatriots, we have an obligation to move decisively to remove all those obstacles which limit our capacity to deal effectively with this scourge. Do we really have any justification for perpetuating such practices as the migrant labour system, single sex hostels, which not only destroy family life, but certainly limit our capacity to establish stable self-reliant communities that can be the core of a dynamic society able to cope with this and other problems? Is it not time we address the problem of illiteracy, poverty and empower our women folk—all crucial factors for an effective intervention strategy?

Very few, if any diseases better illustrate the truth in the dictum "prevention is better than cure".

Lastly, AIDS definitely has profound direct micro and macro-economic impacts. In the years ahead, as we face the process of national reconstruction, we shall need the best possible performance of our national economy. Let us therefore act now to ensure that our efforts at nation building and democratic transformation will not be frustrated.

Speech On Acceptance Of The Prince Of Asturias Prize Of International Co-Operation

October 31, 1992

Your Majesty The Queen, Your Royal Highness The Prince of Asturias, Your excellencies, The President of the Prince of Asturias Foundation, Ladies and Gentlemen:

It is a single and notable honour for me to receive from your Royal Highness, Don Felipe, Prince of Asturias, the Prize for International Co-operation, named after you. This is my third visit to Spain and each has been an occasion for joy and celebration.

In July the world rejoiced with you when Spain hosted the Olympic Games, a spectacular gathering of the world at peace with itself. The ceremonies showed to the world that Spain can unite the old and the new and forge a common identity out of its richness of diverse regions, culture and civilisation.

The world needs peace so that the proud claims in the Charter of the United Nations can be renewed and refashioned to meet the challenges of the future. We must all support the review of the role of the United Nations now being undertaken so that a democratic and stronger United Nations can fulfill the hopes of humanity.

The new international order must not become a cloak for the naked self-interest of powerful states but must be based on solidarity and international law.

During our long years of imprisonment on Robben Island, our real contact with the international community was through the principles of international law and the forums of the United Nations. We were sustained by the support of the international community who, even during the height of the Cold War, by their consensus, united in the rejection of apartheid. It is our great challenge to develop new areas of consensus to consolidate the developments of our era.

The principle of decolonisation and the acceptance of the rights of all nations to belong to and participate equally in the life of the world community must not be debased so as to oppress other peoples.

Further, the acceptance of universally applicable standards of human rights, the enjoyment of which is the right of all human beings must now be strengthened by collective measures under the auspices of the Security Council to avert gross violations of human rights and the crime of all crimes, genocide.

Finally, the international community must, as an urgent priority, establish mechanisms to ensure that the finite resources of our planet are not dissipated.

Africa's heritage of beneficial, cultural, political and social relations with the peoples of other continents is a proud and creative achievement of a human-centred sensibility. We still endeavour to emulate its values. In particular, our relations with Spain, dating back to ancient times, compel us to speculate — what Euro-African culture would have been had Hannibal's elephants reached Rome.

The situation in many parts of the African continent can only be described as calamitous. The spectre of famine, starvation, violence and diseases, such as AIDS, is stalking at a time when science and modern technology are reaching the heights of accomplishment. The international community responds with various forms of aid. We welcome and need this solidarity, with the injunction that what our continent needs, above all, is development, to promote and realise our human potential at its fullest.

The path of peace and justice also depends on the renewal of the North-South debate and the strengthening of international structures of co-operation.

South Africa is preparing to take its rightful place in the international community, no longer as an international pariah but as a country which is about to grasp the challenge of non-racialism and democracy. We must therefore pay our tribute to the international community for its contribution to the struggle against racism and apartheid and, especially, for the sacrifices made by many countries in Africa. Without such solidarity, we would not be walking the last mile to freedom.

A free South Africa must forever remove the spectre of force in its relations with other states.

The policy of a free South Africa will therefore contribute to the democratisation of international political and economic relations. In a changing world, we will support the proposal to declare Africa as a Nuclear-free Zone and the Indian Ocean as a Sea of Peace.

Most importantly, we will play a full and dynamic role in regional and international organisations to help overcome the ravages of apartheid and the destabilisation of our neighbours and to build a world where all are cherished equally. I ask Spain to join in this exciting and bold task.

It gives me great pleasure to accept this prestigious and important award. Thank you.

Negotiations, the ANC Vision of a New South African and the Indian Community

February 13, 1983

Assalaam Ualaikum, Namiste and Good Evening.

We are gathered here today at a time when South Africa is at the threshold of some of the most momentous political changes.

I am advised that this gathering tonight represents some of the most senior business and community leaders of the Indian community throughout the Transvaal. I am honoured to be a part of it and I thank you for this opportunity. This is a most important meeting for the ANC. This is the first opportunity that we have had to address you.

As part of the Black majority in this country, you have hitherto been subjected to the worst forms of discrimination possible. As part of the Black business community in this country, you were further confronted with measures specifically designed to prevent you from equally competing with white business. You were forcefully removed from your places of residence and business, subjected to Group Areas, denied the right to trade where you wanted and in what you wanted and denied the right of access to training in skills and capital that would have allowed you to develop further.

Nevertheless, in spite of all these impediments you have shown the necessary ingenuity and creativeness that has ensured that you are successful in doing what you do best — serving our communities with the necessary goods and services required. The skills that you have gained are invaluable to our country.

In this year of the Gandhi centenary we can proudly declare to our people and the world at large that our history of struggle, in which the Indian community played no small part, is bearing fruit. The strength that we gained from years of resistance to apartheid enabled the ANC to take the initiative and force the NP regime to the negotiating table.

At this auspicious occasion, I am obliged to give a report of the developments in the negotiations process. However, it is also important for me to place before you the ANC vision of a new South Africa and the role of the Indian community.

The Negotiations Process

Firstly, let me dispel all rumours that there have been any secret deals or pacts agreed to with the government. These rumours are devoid of any truth and mischievous in the extreme.

I furthermore wish to categorically deny the statement made in the press that the ANC has agreed to power sharing until the year 1999. An Interim Government of National Unity is not power sharing. What the government has proposed is a form of power sharing. The ANC, on the other hand, proposes an interim Government of National Unity which would include those parties that have won a certain proportion of the seats in the Constituent Assembly. This proposal is designed to create national unity and is not a simple power sharing formula.

The government's proposals merely reflects their struggle for survival, and therefore their insistence merely exposes their self interest. The ANC's proposal, however, clearly shows the priority we have given to national interests above that of our own.

1. The vision of the ANC for the immediate future is as follows:

Firstly, we would like to see an early resumption of multilateral negotiations. In this phase we aim to secure: an agreement on free and fair elections, an Interim Government of National Unity and a sovereign Constituent Assembly; to stop all unilateral restructuring; broaden the space for free political activity; and address the issue of violence.

Secondly, we must secure the establishment of the Transitional Executive Council. In this phase we should aim to: consolidate peace through joint control over all armed formations; ensure free and fair elections; and mobilise for a decisive victory in the elections.

Thirdly, this would allow us to enter the period of the drafting and adoption of the new constitution by the Constituent Assembly It is during this phase that we aim to establish the Interim Government of National Unity, adopt a new constitution and start addressing the socio-economic problems facing our country.

Fourthly, once a new constitution has been adopted, we would have to restructure the present state machinery with a view to dismantling the system of apartheid.

Fifthly, we would then enter a period of the consolidation of the process of democratic transformation and reconstruction.

2. Report on the negotiations process

The objective of the ANC in the present phase of negotiations is to ensure that this country moves as swiftly as possible towards the election of an Interim Government of

National Unity and a Constituent Assembly that would be charged with the responsibility of drafting and adopting a democratic constitution. The unacceptable levels of violence, crime and the deteriorating economy demand that this be so.

Over the last few days our negotiators have been locked in intense bilateral discussions with the regime. The ANC delegation was led by our Secretary General, Cyril Ramaphosa. Roelf Meyer, the NP Minister of Constitutional Development, led the government delegation.

The meeting covered discussions on constitutional questions as well as preparations for the resumption of multi-party negotiations.

The meeting reaffirmed agreement on an elected constitution-making body that would draft and adopt the new constitution. Agreement was also reached that elections for this body would take place as early as possible.

To ensure free and fair elections the following issues were discussed:

Various suggestions relating to various aspects of the legislation establishing Transitional Executive Council were made. There are still to be discussed further and will be finalised in due course. In this regard, the ANC provided the government with concrete proposals on the powers and functions of the TEC, and in particular, its sub-councils for Law and Order and Defence. The government undertook to come back to the ANC on these issues.

Agreement was reached that an Independent Electoral Commission would run the elections. In this regard we have also proposed, and it has been accepted, that international observers and experts would also be involved in the process. Furthermore, there would be an Independent Media Commission would be appointed. These Commissions would play a crucial role in leveling the playing field. These agreements are in line with the ANC's stated positions that both the media and the elections must be free of party political bias or orientation.

On the appointment of the SABC Board, it was agreed that a transparent process should be set in motion. After consultation with a wide range of forces including the Campaign of independent Broadcasting, the ANC has proposed that Justice Ismail Mohammed and Piet Schabbort should be appointed to initiate this process. The government has promised to come back to the ANC on this issue early next week.

At the meeting, the government also raised the question of a possible Government of National Unity extending for a limited period after the adoption of a new constitution. The matter is to be placed before the National Executive Committee for discussion.

Concerning the boundaries, powers and functions of regions, it was agreed that decisions in this regard would only be taken by the elected Constitution Making Body.

Finally, it was agreed that a multi-party planning conference, that would prepare the way for the resumption of multilateral negotiations, would be held during the course of this month. If the government responds positively to the concrete proposals which the ANC placed on the table, the realisation of a peaceful and democratic order is within our reach.

What has become accepted is that the ANC has placed for discussions proposals which are eminently reasonable and which take into account the concerns and fears of the various communities in our country.

Nevertheless, like in so many other countries, the process of transition and political transformation brings with it some measure of uncertainty and perhaps even a sense of insecurity. South Africa is no different and the Indian community here is no exception. All of this, together with the unabating violence, increasing crime and deteriorating economy, not to mention the revelation of one scandal after another involving government, has given rise to a whole host of fears and concerns which are legitimate and understandable.

Whilst you have the right to choose which political party or organisation would best serve your interests, there is little choice as to how to deal with and confront all those fears and concerns. It is against this background that I make the following call to you:

As a community and population group, you have a proud tradition and history of resistance against injustice and the struggle for democracy. Maintain this and strengthen it.

There are only two key political role players in this country. The ANC and the NP. The National Party, on the one hand, has a history of discrimination, oppression, exploitation. It is also so arrogant that it continues to believe it knows what is best for your community. That is why it will refuse to consult you on developments in this country. On the other hand, it is only the African National Congress that has consistently consulted all communities on all major issues. This is even true of the formation of Umkhonto We Sizwe in 1960. Then, the Indian Congresses were consulted before the decision was taken.

The forthcoming election will be the first time that all South Africans would vote as equals. Above all it would be no ordinary election. It would be an election of delegates of whom the people would entrust to draft and adopt a new democratic constitution for unified South Africa. In this way we would get a constitution that would give expression to the aspirations of all our peoples whatever their colour, class or creed. It is in this constitution where we could best ensure the protection of religious, cultural and political freedoms. These elections are therefore of special importance to our country because it would shape the nature of our country and society for generations to come. The future of our children is being shaped now. It is therefore necessary to ensure that we mobilise our entire communities to vote. Leaders such as yourselves present here tonight could make this a reality. It is necessary that you also call house meetings, meetings of business people, other structures and the community, and invite ANC leaders from our branches, regions and even the head office to discuss various issues with you. This would ensure that the process of consultation carried out by the ANC is more rigorous.

You will have been given copies of the ANC's policy guidelines. These are not final policies. They are merely guidelines which need to be developed further. To this extent it is necessary to consider these proposals and engage the structures of the ANC in discussion so as to ensure that the interests of the Indian community are well considered.

You will note that it is the policy of the ANC to ensure that we provide the necessary incentives to ensure that our business people are allowed to develop so as to allow them to compete equally with their white counterparts. Unless we are able to build on the skills developed amongst your business people and secure that black business people are empowered to break into the industrial and manufacturing sectors, this economy would continue to be monopolised by a few white conglomerates. It is therefore in our interest to ensure that black business not only prosper but grow. To do this, we will need your assistance to ensure that we develop an effective economic strategy.

Finally, it is necessary that you continue with the generous financial assistance that you have thus far provided us with. However, we also need human resources. In this regard, leaders such as yourselves are invaluable and are able to assist in using your influence to convince your communities to involve themselves in the process of transformation that is unfolding. After all, the best way to deal with your fears and concerns brought on by the transformation is to ensure that you are part of the process that manages it.

Before I conclude, I wish to convey my warmest greetings to all Muslims who will be engaged in fasting during the holy month of Ramadan. May you also have a happy Eid.

In conclusion, I sincerely hope that all goes well with your preparations for the Gandhi Centenary celebrations. There are many lessons that one could draw on from the proud history of Gandhiji, and I hope that these would place you in good stead in dealing with this unfolding process of transition.

I thank you.

Speech To Members Of The British Parliament

May 5, 1993

Chairperson, My Lords, Distinguished Members of Parliament, Ladies and Gentlemen:

I would like to thank the Conservative Party and Labour Party's Foreign Affairs Committee for the honour they extended to us by inviting us to be with you today. We are conscious of the fact that the buildings where we are today represent a political history which reaches back through many centuries.

They symbolise past heroic struggles against tyranny and autocracy. They have meaning because, long before today, there was a determined striving to ensure that the people shall govern.

These Houses of Parliament remain today living structures, because, whatever the imperfections of your political system — and there must be many — these structures continue to provide a seat for the furtherance of the humane perspective that the natural conflict of interests, ideas and instincts among any people, can and should be expressed through peaceful struggle rather than through actions which are predicated on violence and death.

I say these things because our own country and people are striving to create a social order, as well as establish the institutions, that will ensure that we, too, resolve the natural conflict of interests, ideas and instincts among ourselves through a peaceful contest rather than through the pursuit of policies whose success is measured by the success of terror.

But I also speak thus, within this historic enclave, because, hidden by the dim mists of history, there is also the reality that, from here, there issued decisions which imposed on my own country and people a condition of existence which condemned us, as South Africans, to seek to resolve our conflicts not through peaceful means but by other than peaceful means.

Your right to determine your own destiny was used to deny us to determine our own.

Thus history brought our peoples together in its own peculiar ways. That history demands of us that we should strive to achieve what you, through the rediscovery of the practice of democracy, achieved for yourselves.

It demands of you that you should assist us, and therefore yourselves as well, to rediscover for ourselves, as a people, the practice of democracy.

And I say "demands" not because I want to entrust to you the role of a guardian and impose on ourselves the condition of an innocent ward.

I say history demands of you that you help us achieve a speedy transition to a non-racial and non-sexist democracy because your very national interest requires that you do so.

This, history has decreed, and not the sentimental heart of an old man.

My Lords, Ladies and Gentleman:

The universe we inhabit as human beings is becoming a common home that shows growing disrespect for the rigidities imposed on humanity by national boundaries.

These much used words of one of your great poets, John Donne, speak to what we are trying to say:

"No Man is an Island, entire of itself; Every man is a piece of the Continent, A part of the main."

South Africa and the former Yugoslavia, Somalia and Angola, Liberia and Nagorno Kharabakh, the Sudan and Northern Ireland, are all part of the main.

The evil that occurs in any of these places diminishes us all and the good elevates all humanity.

Many peoples across the globe are hurt, and their rights to independence and sovereignty undermined, when you who are relatively wealthy, attach certain conditionalities to any economic assistance to those who are poor, such as the establishment of democratic systems, respect for human rights, reduction of military expenditures and resolution of disputes by peaceful means. But, as Africans, we too believe that we should, together, transform our continent into one that is governed according to these precepts.

Therefore, between us, there is no difference as to the objectives that must be achieved. There may however be differences about the means that must be used and the route to travel to arrive at these common goals.

But, once more, these processes emphasize precisely the point about the ever-growing interdependence among the peoples.

South Africa has been on your national agenda in various ways since the 17th Century, when the ships of the English East India Company sailed around the Cape.

In more recent times, and with regard to South Africa, the great pre-occupation of members of these Houses of Parliament, the British Government and the public at large has been with the issue of apartheid.

This country has produced men and women whose names are well known in South Africa, because they, together with thousands of others of your citizens, stood up to oppose this evil system and helped to bring us to where we are today, when we can say — at last, freedom is in sight.

These Britons acted in the way they did because they realised that they and their country had as much a moral obligation and a strategic imperative to uproot the pernicious system of racism in South Africa, as they had to destroy a similar system in Nazi Germany.

We firmly believe that, through their struggles, these, your compatriots, have established the fundamental point that you and the people you represent have an obligation to act together with us as we strive to give birth to a new South Africa.

The agenda for that process of transforming South Africa has a number of items that stand out in bold relief. These are:

the determination of an Election date;

the creation of a climate conducive to free and fair elections, including the establishment of a multi-party Transitional Executive Council, an Independent Electoral Commission and an Independent Media Commission;

the holding of the first ever general elections in our country, based on the principle of one person one vote, and thus ending the system of white minority rule;

as a consequence of these elections, the formation of an elected constituent assembly to draft a democratic constitution;

as a second consequence of these elections, the formation of an Interim Government of National Unity that will include all the political organisations that will have demonstrated that they have significant support;

the implementation of programmes aimed at dismantling the system of apartheid and reconstructing South Africa into a truly united, democratic, non-racial and non-sexist country;

the rebuilding and the restructuring of its economy to ensure rapid growth, more equitable distribution of income, wealth and opportunities, and an end to poverty as well as racial and gender inequalities; and,

the normalisation of South Africa's relations with the rest of the world.

We would like you to play a role with regard to all these processes.

First among them is your contribution to ensuring that all political actors in South Africa understand that the situation in the country demands a speedy transition to a non-racial democracy. There should be no further delay in agreeing an election date.

We request that you use such contact as you have with political actors to persuade them to abandon their selfish and sectarian positions and stop blocking movement forward.

We would further urge you to use your influence to ensure the earliest possible establishment of the Transitional Executive Council and the related Commissions so that all the political parties and organisations in our country can, inter alia, begin to attend jointly to such matters as ending political violence and implementing poverty alleviation programmes.

As you are aware, political violence in South Africa continues to be a matter of grave concern. If anybody had any doubt about how serious the issue is, the recent brutal assassination of one of our outstanding leaders, Chris Hani, should have put paid to these doubts.

We take very seriously the repeated reports we get that good numbers of our leaders and activists have been put on death lists by white right wing groups, whether they are within or outside the sate security force, that are opposed to change and are prepared to take lives to ensure the perpetuation of the apartheid system.

We ourselves are doing everything in our power to address this matter. It is nevertheless incontestable that the government of the day has to do a lot more to deal with this matter and so must other parties. As we have said, we are also convinced that the establishment of the Transitional Executive Council with its structures for multi-party control of all armed formations and the police would make a decisive contribution in helping us to contain and reduce the level of violence.

Accordingly, we urge that you put pressure on those concerned within South Africa to carry out their obligations with regard to this matter of violence.

We would like to take this opportunity to express our appreciation for the role that this country has already played with regard to this matter, by sending police officers and other experts into South Africa and by the contributions it has made through the United Nations, The Commonwealth and the European Community.

When the elections are held, it will be important that the international community place observers in South Africa to help us ensure that the elections are free and fair and therefore that their outcome is recognised by everybody as being legitimate and acceptable.

We are certain that you will play your part in helping us benefit from such international assistance.

Three years ago we emerged from 30 years of illegality, during which much of our leadership was imprisoned or exiled and the members inside the country forced to operate as clandestine units.

In addition to this, precisely because the majority had been denied the right to vote, we suffer from the added disadvantage that we have no experience of elections, of parliamentary practice, and of state administration.

And yet I dare say that stability cannot be achieved in South Africa unless the ANC, which represents the overwhelming majority of our people, plays a central role in bringing these masses into the peace process, organising that they go to the polls in their millions and ensuring that any constitution and government that result from these processes are accepted as being expressive of the will of the people.

The fact that we, like other political formations, will participate in the elections, does not therefore remove the obligation on the international community to assist us and the rest of the democratic movement of our country, both materially and politically.

Indeed, I would venture to say that the process of change enhances the need to strengthen this democratic movement and not the other way round.

I am certain that many of you in this room will recognise the relevance and correctness of what I am saying from your experiences here in Europe.

The processes of democratic transformation in such countries as Spain, Portugal and Greece could not have been as relatively smooth as they were without relatively strong democratic political organisations.

The same lesson is now being confirmed in other parts of Europe, again demonstrating that democratic change requires democratic organisations.

We trust that you will respond to these observations as they affect South Africa positively, and open yourselves to persuasion that, in the common interest, you should extend all-round assistance to us.

As you know, in 1989 the United Nations General Assembly adopted a Consensus Declaration on Southern Africa, with the active participation of the British government. That Declaration has provided the broad framework for the process of negotiations in South Africa.

It includes within it a set of principles which the international community thought had to be implemented to provide the basis for an international acceptable solution of the South African question.

Accordingly we would urge that you should maintain such pressure as is necessary until we do indeed arrive at this international acceptable solution.

There can be no gainsaying the point that the very survival of the democratic settlement towards which we strive cannot be guaranteed unless we address speedily and successfully the socio-economic upliftment of the majority of our people.

Central to this is the achievement of a relatively high rate of growth of the South African economy. We hope that British Companies will participate in this process, to the mutual benefit, by investing directly to raise the level of capital formation, help modernise our economy through the transfer of technology, open the way to new markets, and create new jobs to absorb the millions of the unemployed.

We also hope that both your public and private sectors will help us to address the urgent issues of education and training, in particular to raise the levels of productivity without which it would be impossible to have a modern and an internationally competitive economy.

Together, we have to confront another particular matter which has to do with a false perception of what South Africa is.

This has to do with our classification as a middle income country. This impacts on the issue whether we can receive overseas development assistance or not.

The actual reality of South Africa is, that, beyond the aggregate statistics, the majority of our population, which happens to be black, lives in conditions of dire poverty.

The situation which these millions face is not only catastrophic in quantitative terms, but also of a crisis nature in a qualitative and structural sense.

In reality, we face a situation of the coexistence within one country of a first world and a third world economy.

The aggregate statistics disguise the reality of structural poverty and endemic underdevelopment to which the majority of the population is condemned.

This is possible because so rich are the few that are rich, that it becomes impossible to see that the poor exist at all.

We raise this matter because it will be necessary that we get your support to persuade the OECD, GATT, the UNDP and similar organisations, that in dealing with South Africa, we are dealing with a developing country.

As you know, this is critically relevant to the issue of how you and other developed countries will handle such issues as development assistance, soft loans and market access, as they relate to a democratic South Africa.

Related to this is the challenge to define the relationship between democratic South Africa and the European Community, our largest international economic partner.

To arrive at the correct framework with regard to this matter will require that you, as parliamentarians who understand what needs to be done really to end the system of apartheid, should use your influence and the influence of your parties to get the European Community to enter into a mutually beneficial agreement with the new South Africa, as soon as is practicable and feasible.

With regard to these socio-economic matters, we are also convinced that it is important that the mass anti-apartheid movement of this country should, in addition to opposing the apartheid system and maintaining the pressure for speedy movement forward to democratic change, also look for ways and means by which it could assist with regard to the developmental issues that face us.

We are therefore very keen that there should be established person-to-person relations between our peoples, so that those who spent their lives fighting the apartheid system should, at the non-governmental level, use their considerable energies to generate the resources which will enable the ordinary people of this country to remain engaged in the struggle to make South Africa into the country which all of us would like it to be.

We are convinced that a genuinely democratic South Africa will be your reliable partner as the international community continue to grapple with such critical matters as a democratic world order, human rights, development, peace, and the protection of the environment.

We therefore believe that it is as much in your interest as ours to ensure that we move forward as speedily as possible to arrive at the point where we do indeed become a democratic country.

A few days ago we bade farewell to a man very dear to me, our former President, Oliver Tambo, who many of you knew.

I was very pleased and moved by the presence of very high level international delegations at Oliver's funeral.

Their participation in this dignified and solemn occasion was both befitting the status of Oliver Tambo and also said to us that the peoples of the world remain true to their pledge that they will stand with us until the apartheid crime against humanity is a thing of the past.

We count you among these millions who are true friends and dependable allies.

Thank you.

Statement At The United Nations

September 24, 1993

Chairperson; Your Excellencies, Ambassadors to the United Nations; Ladies and gentlemen:

We are most grateful to the Special Committee against Apartheid and its distinguished Chairman, His Excellency Professor Ibrahim Gambari, as well as the United Nations as a whole, for enabling us to address this gathering today.

We have, together, walked a very long road. We have traveled together to reach a common destination.

The common destination towards which we have been advancing defines the very reason for the existence of this world Organisation.

The goal we have sought to reach is the consummation of the yearning of all humankind for human dignity and human fulfillment.

For that reason, we have been outraged and enraged that there could be imposed on any people the criminal system of apartheid.

Each and every one of us have felt our humanity denied by the mere existence of this system. Each and every one of us have felt brandished as sub-human by the fact that some could treat of others as though they were no more than disposable garbage.

In the end, there was nobody of conscience who could stand by and do nothing in the search for an end to the apartheid crime against humanity.

We are here today to convey to you, who are the representatives of the peoples of the world, the profound gratitude of the people of South Africa for your engagement, over the decades, in the common struggle to end the system of apartheid.

We are deeply moved by the fact that almost from its birth, this Organisation has kept on its agenda the vital question of the liquidation of the system of apartheid and white minority rule in our country.

Throughout the many years of struggle, we, as South Africans, have been greatly inspired and strengthened as you took action both severally and collectively, to escalate your offensive against apartheid rule, as the white minority regime itself took new steps in its own offensive further to entrench its illegitimate rule and draw tribute from those it had enslaved.

In particular, we are most grateful for the measures that the United Nations, the OAU, the Commonwealth, the Non-Aligned Movement, the European Community and other intergovernmental organisations took to isolate apartheid South Africa.

We are deeply appreciative of similar initiatives that individual countries, non-governmental organisations, local communities and even single individuals took, as part of their contribution to the common effort to deny the apartheid system all international sustenance.

This global struggle, perhaps without precedent in the inestimable number of people it united around one common issue, has helped decisively to bring us to where we are today.

Finally, the apartheid regime was forced to concede that the system of white minority rule could no longer be sustained.

It was forced to accept that it had to enter into negotiations with the genuine representatives of our people to arrive at a solution which, as agreed at the first sitting of the Convention for a Democratic South Africa, CODESA, would transform South Africa into a united, democratic, non-racial and non-sexist country.

This and other agreements have now been translated into a specific programme that will enable our country to take a leap forward from its dark, painful and turbulent past to a glorious future, which our people will strive with all their strength to make a future of democracy, peace, stability and prosperity.

The countdown to democracy in South Africa has begun. The date for the demise of the white minority regime has been determined, agreed and set.

Seven months from now, on April 27, 1994, all the people of South Africa, without discrimination on grounds of gender, race, colour or belief, will join in the historic act of electing a government of their choice.

The legislation has also been passed to create the institutions of state, the statutory organs that will ensure that these elections are held and that they are free and fair.

As a consequence of the creation of these statutory instruments, we have arrived at the point where our country will no longer be governed exclusively by a white minority regime.

The Transitional Executive Council, provided for in this legislation, will mark the first ever participation by the majority of our people at governmental level in the process of determining the destiny of our country.

It will be the historic precursor to the Interim Government of National Unity which will be formed after the democratic elections of April 27th.

The other structures now provided for in law, the Independent Election Commission, the Independent Media Commission and the Independent Broadcasting Authority, will themselves play their specified roles in ensuring a process of transition and a result which our people as a whole will accept as having been legitimate and therefore acceptable.

We must however warn that we are not yet out of the woods.

Negotiations are continuing, to agree on the interim constitution according to which the country will be governed as the elected national assembly works on the final constitution.

There will therefore be a continuing need that this Organisation and the world movement for a democratic South Africa as a whole, sustain their focus on the transitional processes, so that everybody concerned in our country is left in no doubt about the continuing determination of the international community to help see us through to democracy.

The reality is that there are various forces within South Africa which do not accept the inevitability of the common outcome which all humanity seeks.

Within our country, these forces, which seek to deny us liberty by resort to brute force, and which have already murdered and maimed people in their tens of thousands, represent a minority of the people.

They derive their strength not from the people but from the fear, insecurity and destabilisation which they seek to impose through a campaign of terrorism conducted by unknown killers whose hallmark is brutality and total disregard for the value of human life.

There are other forces, which because of narrow, sectarian interests, are also opposed to genuine change. These are engaged in other actions which seek to create obstacles on the way to a smooth transition to democracy.

We believe that it is critically important that these forces too should understand that the international community has the will and determination to act in concert with the majority of the people of our country, to ensure that the democratic change which is long overdue is not delayed.

The apartheid system has left a swathe of disaster in its trail. We have an economy that is tottering on the brink of an even deeper depression than the one we are experiencing now.

What this means practically is millions of people who have no food, no jobs and no houses.

The very fabric of society is threatened by a process of disintegration, characterised by high and increasing rates of violent crime, the growth in the numbers of people so brutalised that they will kill for a pittance, and the collapse of all social norms.

In addition, the absence of a legitimate state authority, enjoying the support of the majority of the people, immensely exacerbates this general crisis, emphasizing the critical importance of speedy movement forward to democratic change.

In sum, acting together, we must, at all costs, resist and rebuff any tendency of a slide towards another Somalia or a Bosnia, a development which would have disastrous repercussions extending far beyond the borders of South Africa.

What we have just said is not intended to alarm this august gathering. Rather, it is meant to say—now is the time to take new steps to move us forward to the common victory we have all fought for!

We believe the moment has come when the United Nations Organisation and the international community as a whole should take stock of the decisive advances that have been made to create the setting for the victory of the cause of democracy in our country.

We further believe that the moment has come when this same community should lay the basis for halting the slide to a socio-economic disaster in South Africa, as one of the imperatives in ensuring the very success of the democratic transformation itself.

In response to the historic advances towards democracy that have been achieved; further to give added impetus to this process; to strengthen the forces of democratic change and to help create the necessary conditions for stability and social progress, we believe the time has come when the international community should lift all economic sanctions against South Africa.

We therefore extend an earnest appeal to you, the governments and peoples you represent, to take all necessary measures to end the economic sanctions you imposed and which have brought us to the point where the transition to democracy has now been enshrined in the law of our country.

We further urge that this historic step, marking a turning point in the history of the relations between South Africa and the rest of the world, should not be viewed as an act of abstention but one of engagement.

Let us all treat this new reality as an opportunity and a challenge to engage with the South African situation in a way that will advance the democratic cause and create the best possible social and economic conditions for the victory of that cause.

The Special Committee Against Apartheid has itself led the process of preparing the United Nations and its specialised agencies for the new reality that is the fruit of our common struggle. We trust that the UN family will therefore not delay in engaging the people of South Africa in a new way.

We trust also that the governments across the globe, that have been so central in the effort to defeat the system of apartheid, will do what they can to help us ensure the upliftment of our people.

A similar appeal extends the millions of people organised in the broad non-governmental anti-apartheid movement themselves to remain involved in the continuing struggle for a democratic South Africa, and to add to their programmes the extension of all-round development assistance from people to people.

We hope that both the South African and the international investor communities will also take this opportunity themselves to help regenerate the South African economy, to the mutual benefit.

As you know, our people have not yet elected a democratic government. It is therefore important that the white minority government which remains in place in our country should not be granted recognition and treated as though it were representative of all the people of South Africa.

The Transitional Executive Council provides the appropriate mechanism for such interaction as should take place between ourselves and the international community in the period between now and the formation of the new government.

We should here mention that within the ambit of the diplomatic sanctions which many countries imposed, we also believe that such countries may now establish a diplomatic presence in South Africa to enhance their capacity to assist the people of our country to realise the common objectives.

This Organisation also imposed special sanctions relating to arms, nuclear matters, and oil.

In this regard, we would like to urge that the mandatory sanctions be maintained until the new government has been formed. We would leave the issue of the oil embargo to the discretion of the Committee of the General Assembly responsible for the enforcement of this particular sanction.

We would further like to request that the Security Council should begin consideration of the very important issue of what this Organisation should do to assist in the process of organising for and ensuring that the forthcoming elections are indeed free and fair.

This, naturally, should be accompanied by a review of the important contribution that has been made by the UN Observer Mission to South Africa, which is helping us to address the issue of political violence, to ensure that this contribution addresses adequately this continuing problem.

We cannot close without extending our congratulations to the PLO and the government of Israel for the important step forward they have taken which, hopefully, will lead to a just and lasting settlement of the Middle East question.

To them, and to the peoples and governments of the region as a whole, we extend the good wishes of all the people of our country and the assurance of our support for their noble effort to establish justice and peace.

We continue to hope that progress will be made towards the just resolution of the outstanding issue of Western Sahara.

Angola continues to bleed. We urge this Organisation and especially the Security Council to leave no stone unturned to ensure that the killing ends and the democratic process is respected.

We are encouraged by the steps that have been taken to bring peace to Mozambique and trust that no new obstacles will emerge to deny the people of this sister country the peace, stability and prosperity which they have been denied for so long.

Our common victory, against the only system to be declared a crime against humanity since the defeat of nazism, is in sight.

The historic need to end this crime as speedily and peacefully as possible requires that we, the peoples of the world, should remain as united as we have been and as committed as we have been to the cause of democracy, peace, human dignity and prosperity for all the people of South Africa.

Standing among you today, we continue to be moved by the selfless solidarity you have extended to our people. We are aware that by our common actions we have sought not only the liberation of the people of South Africa but also the extension of the frontiers of democracy, non-racialism, non-sexism and human solidarity throughout the world.

Understanding that, we undertake before you all that we will not rest until the noble cause which unites us all emerges triumphant, and a new South Africa fully rejoins the rest of the international community as a country which we can all be proud of.

Thank you.

Statement On The Announcement Of The Award Of The Nobel Peace Prize

October 15, 1993.

Today's announcement that I have been named to receive this most prestigious award for peace was a deeply humbling experience. The Nobel Peace Prize is amongst the highest accolades that can be bestowed on any human being. To be chosen from amongst the millions of deserving men and women throughout the world is a singular honour to which grave responsibilities are attached.

This is the third occasion since the end of the Second World War that our country has been so recognised. I would like to use this occasion to pay tribute to those other great South Africans who have been past recipients of the Peace Prize: Chief Albert J. Luthuli—an outstanding leader of our people and past President of the African National Congress; and that great son of our country who fought so selflessly against the evils of racism during the darkest days of apartheid repression, Archbishop Desmond Mpilo Tutu.

That South Africa has once again been given the Nobel Peace Prize is a tribute to all South Africans. It is an expression of the profound confidence the international community has vested in us that we can collectively address the enormous problems our country faces without recourse to violence and coercion. This is a prize won in the first instance by all those who have, over the decades, struggled so steadfastly for democracy and peace, in the teeth of ruthless and brutal repression. This coveted honour is a challenge to us all as co-equal compatriots to so conduct ourselves that those who seek to foster racial and ethnic hatred and war are isolated and cauterized.

I am keenly aware that the Nobel Peace Prize imposes an even greater obligation on me personally to strive even harder, in the interests of all South Africans, for peace, justice and democracy.

But this is a burden I hope to share with my co-recipient, State President F.W. de Klerk. I extend my heartfelt congratulations to him for this illustrious award and express the hope that we can jointly work towards a future in which the children of South Africa can grow up with the right to a life full of opportunities in a country that recognises, defends and protects the human worth of each and every individual.

There is very little we can give to reciprocate the esteem showered upon us by the world community today. What we can do is to ensure that the negotiation process is successfully concluded, that the agreements reached are adhered to by us all, so that the first democratic elections take place on the 27th of April 1994, as scheduled. The people of South Africa have waited too long for a government elected by all the people. We must not and we dare not fail them. A democratic government, so elected, can and will address the terrible legacy of apartheid and allow every man, woman and child to walk tall, free and proud in the country of their birth.

I dedicate this award to all the courageous people of my country, black and white, who have suffered and endured so much, and pledge that in whatever time remains to me I will spare no effort to bring peace, freedom and justice for all to South Africa.

Acceptance Speech At The Nobel Peace Prize Award Ceremony

December 10, 1993

Your Majesty the King, Your Royal Highness, Honourable Prime Minister, Madame Gro Brundtland, Ministers, Members of Parliament and Ambassadors, Esteemed Members of the Norwegian Nobel Committee, Fellow Laureate, Mr. F.W. de Klerk, Distinguished guests, Friends, ladies and gentlemen:

I am indeed truly humbled to be standing here today to receive this year's Nobel Peace Prize.

I extend my heartfelt thanks to the Norwegian Nobel Committee for elevating us to the status of a Nobel Peace Prize winner.

I would also like to take this opportunity to congratulate my compatriot and fellow laureate, State President F.W. de Klerk, on his receipt of this high honour.

Together, we join two distinguished South Africans, the late Chief Albert Luthuli, and His Grace Archbishop Desmond Tutu, to whose seminal contributions to the peaceful struggle against the evil system of apartheid you paid well-deserved tribute by awarding them the Nobel Peace Prize.

It will not be presumptuous of us if we also add, among our predecessors, the name of another outstanding Nobel Peace Prize winner, the late African-American statesman and internationalist, the Rev Martin Luther King Jr.

He, too, grappled with and died in the effort to make a contribution to the just solution of the same great issues of the day which we have had to face as South Africans.

We speak here of the challenge of the dichotomies of war and peace, violence and non-violence, racism and human dignity, oppression and repression and liberty and human rights, poverty and freedom from want.

We stand here today as nothing more than a representative of the millions of our people who dared to rise up against a social system whose very essence is war, violence, racism, oppression, repression and the impoverishment of an entire people.

I am also here today as a representative of the millions of people across the globe, the anti-apartheid movement, the governments and organisations that joined with us, not to fight against South Africa as a country or any of its peoples, but to oppose an inhuman system and sue for a speedy end to the apartheid crime against humanity.

These countless human beings, both inside and outside our country, had the nobility of spirit to stand in the path of tyranny and injustice, without seeking selfish gain. They recognised that an injury to one is an injury to all and therefore acted together in defence of justice and a common human decency.

Because of their courage and persistence for many years, we can, today, even set the dates when all humanity will join together to celebrate one of the outstanding human victories of our century.

When that moment comes, we shall, together, rejoice in a common victory over racism, apartheid and white minority rule.

That triumph will finally bring to a close a history of five hundred years of African colonisation that began with the establishment of the Portuguese empire.

Thus, it will mark a great step forward in history and also serve as a common pledge of the peoples of the world to fight racism wherever it occurs and whatever guise it assumes.

At the southern tip of the continent of Africa, a rich reward is in the making, an invaluable gift is in the preparation, for those who suffered in the name of all humanity when they sacrificed everything—for liberty, peace, human dignity and human fulfillment.

This reward will not be measured in money. Nor can it be reckoned in the collective price of the rare metals and precious stones that rest in the bowels of the African soil we tread in the footsteps of our ancestors. It will and must be measured by the happiness and welfare of the children, at once the most vulnerable citizens in any society and the greatest of our treasures.

The children must, at last, play in the open veld, no longer tortured by the pangs of hunger or ravaged by disease or threatened with the scourge of ignorance, molestation and abuse, and no longer required to engage in deeds whose gravity exceeds the demands of their tender years.

In front of this distinguished audience, we commit the new South Africa to the relentless pursuit of the purposes defined in the World Declaration on the Survival, Protection and Development of Children.

The reward of which we have spoken will and must also be measured by the happiness and welfare of the mothers and fathers of these children, who must walk the earth without fear of being robbed, killed for political or material profit, or spat upon because they are beggars.

They too must be relieved of the heavy burden of despair which they carry in their hearts, born of hunger, homelessness and unemployment.

The value of that gift to all who have suffered will and must be measured by the happiness and welfare of all the people of our country, who will have torn down the inhuman walls that divide them.

These great masses will have turned their backs on the grave insult to human dignity which described some as masters and others as servants, and transformed each into a predator whose survival depended on the destruction of the other.

The value of our shared reward will and must be measured by the joyful peace which will triumph, because the common humanity that bonds both black and white into one human race, will have said to each one of us that we shall all live like the children of paradise.

Thus shall we live, because we will have created a society which recognises that all people are born equal, with each entitled in equal measure to life, liberty, prosperity, human rights and good governance.

Such a society should never allow again that there should be prisoners of conscience, nor that any person's human rights should be violated.

Neither should it ever happen that once more the avenues to peaceful change are blocked by usurpers who seek to take power away from the people, in pursuit of their own ignoble purposes.

In relation to these matters, we appeal to those who govern Burma that they release our fellow Nobel Peace Prize laureate, Aung San Suu Kyi, and engage her and those she represents in serious dialogue, for the benefit of all the people of Burma.

We pray that those who have the power to do so will, without further delay, permit that she uses her talents and energies for the greater good of the people of her country and humanity as a whole.

Far from the rough and tumble of the politics of our own country, I would like to take this opportunity to join the Norwegian Nobel Committee and pay tribute to my joint laureate, Mr. F.W. de Klerk.

He had the courage to admit that a terrible wrong had been done to our country and people through the imposition of the system of apartheid.

He had the foresight to understand and accept that all the people of South Africa must, through negotiations and as equal participants in the process, together determine what they want to make of their future.

But there are still some within our country who wrongly believe they can make a contribution to the cause of justice and peace by clinging to the shibboleths that have been proved to spell nothing but disaster.

It remains our hope that these, too, will be blessed with sufficient reason to realise that history will not be denied, and that the new society cannot be created by reproducing the repugnant past, however refined or enticingly repackaged.

We live with the hope that as she battles to remake herself, South Africa will be like a microcosm of the new world that is striving to be born.

This must be a world of democracy and respect for human rights, a world freed from the horrors of poverty, hunger, deprivation and ignorance, relieved of the threat and the scourge of civil wars and external aggression and unburdened of the great tragedy of millions forced to become refugees.

The processes in which South Africa and Southern Africa as a whole are engaged, beckon and urge us all that we take this tide at the flood and make of this region a living example of what all people of conscience would like the world to be.

We do not believe that this Nobel Peace Prize is intended as a commendation for matters that have happened and passed.

We hear the voices which say that it is an appeal from all those, throughout the universe, who sought an end to the system of apartheid.

We understand their call, that we devote what remains of our lives to the use of our country's unique and painful experience to demonstrate, in practice, that the normal condition for human existence is democracy, justice, peace, non-racism, non-sexism, prosperity for everybody, a healthy environment, and equality and solidarity among the peoples.

Moved by that appeal and inspired by the eminence you have thrust upon us, we undertake that we too will do what we can to contribute to the renewal of our world so that none should, in future, be described as the wretched of the earth.

Let it never be said by future generations that indifference, cynicism or selfishness made us fail to live up to the ideals of humanism which the Nobel Peace Prize encapsulates.

Let the strivings of us all, prove Martin Luther King Jr to have been correct, when he said that humanity can no longer be tragically bound to the starless midnight of racism and war.

Let the efforts of us all, prove that he was not a mere dreamer when he spoke of the beauty of genuine brotherhood and peace being more precious than diamonds or silver or gold.

Let a new age dawn!

Thank you.

Speech Announcing The ANC Election Victory

May 2, 1994

My fellow South Africans — the people of South Africa:

This is indeed a joyous night. Although not yet final, we have received the provisional results of the election, and are delighted by the overwhelming support for the African National Congress.

To all those in the African National Congress and the democratic movement who worked so hard these last few days and through these many decades, I thank you and honour you. To the people of South Africa and the world who are watching: this a joyous night for the human spirit. This is your victory too. You helped end apartheid, you stood with us through the transition.

I watched, along with all of you, as the tens of thousands of our people stood patiently in long queues for many hours. Some sleeping on the open ground overnight waiting to cast this momentous vote.

South Africa's heroes are legend across the generations. But it is you, the people, who are our true heroes.

This is one of the most important moments in the life of our country. I stand here before you filled with deep pride and joy — pride in the ordinary, humble people of this country. You have shown such a calm, patient determination to reclaim this country as your own. And joy that we can loudly proclaim from the rooftops — free at last!

I stand before you humbled by your courage, with a heart full of love for all of you. I regard it as the highest honour to lead the ANC at this moment in our history, and that we have been chosen to lead our country into the new century.

I pledge to use all my strength and ability to live up to your expectations of me as well as of the ANC.

I am personally indebted and pay tribute to some of South Africa's greatest leaders including John Dube, Josiah Gumede, GM Naicker, Dr Abduraman, Chief Lutuli, Lilian Ngoyi, Helen Joseph, Yusuf Dadoo, Moses Kotane, Chris Hani, and Oliver Tambo. They should have been here to celebrate with us, for this is their achievement too.

Tomorrow, the entire ANC leadership and I will be back at our desks. We are rolling up our sleeves to begin tackling the problems our country faces. We ask you all to join us — go back to your jobs in the morning. Let's get South Africa working.

For we must, together and without delay, begin to build a better life for all South Africans. This means creating jobs building houses, providing education and bringing peace and security for all.

The calm and tolerant atmosphere that prevailed during the elections depicts the type of South Africa we can build. It set the tone for the future. We might have our differences, but we are one people with a common destiny in our rich variety of culture, race and tradition.

People have voted for the party of their choice and we respect that. This is democracy.

I hold out a hand of friendship to the leaders of all parties and their members, and ask all of them to join us in working together to tackle the problems we face as a nation. An ANC government will serve all the people of South Africa, not just ANC members.

We also commend the security forces for the sterling work done. This has laid a solid foundation for a truly professional security force, committed to the service of the people and loyalty to the new constitution.

Now is the time for celebration, for South Africans to join together to celebrate the birth of democracy. I raise a glass to you all for working so hard to achieve what can only be called a small miracle. Let our celebrations be in keeping with the mood set in the elections, peaceful, respectful and disciplined, showing we are a people ready to assume the responsibilities of government.

I promise that I will do my best to be worthy of the faith and confidence you have placed in me and my organisation, the African National Congress. Let us build the future together, and toast a better life for all South Africans.

Address On The Occasion Of Inauguration As State President

May 9, 1994

Mr Master of Ceremonies, Your Excellencies, Members of the Diplomatic Corps, My Fellow South Africans:

Today we are entering a new era for our country and its people. Today we celebrate not the victory of a party, but a victory for all the people of South Africa.

Our country has arrived at a decision. Among all the parties that contested the elections, the overwhelming majority of South Africans have mandated the African National Congress to lead our country into the future. The South Africa we have struggled for, in which all our people, be they African, Coloured, Indian or White, regard themselves as citizens of one nation, is at hand.

Perhaps it was history that ordained that it be here, at the Cape of Good Hope, that we should lay the foundation stone of our new nation. For it was here at this Cape, over three centuries ago, that there began the fateful convergence of the peoples of Africa, Europe, and Asia on these shores.

It was to this peninsula that the patriots, among them many princes and scholars, of Indonesia, were dragged in chains. It was on the sandy plains of this peninsula that first battles of the epic wars of resistance were fought.

When we look out across Table Bay, the horizon is dominated by Robben Island, whose infamy as a dungeon built to stifle the spirit of freedom is as old as colonialism in South Africa. For three centuries that island was seen as a place to which outcasts can be banished. The names of those who were incarcerated on Robben Island is a roll call of resistance fighters and democrats spanning over three centuries. If indeed this is a Cape of Good Hope, that hope owes much to the spirit of that legion of fighters and others of their calibre.

We have fought for a democratic constitution since the 1880s. Ours has been a quest for a constitution freely adopted by the people of South Africa, reflecting their wishes and their aspirations. The struggle for democracy has never been a matter pursued by one race, class, religious community or gender among South Africans. In honouring those who fought to see this day arrive, we honour the best sons and daughters of all our people. We can count amongst them Africans, Coloureds, Whites, Indians, Muslims, Christians, Hindus, Jews — all of them united by a common vision of a better life for the people of this country.

It was that vision that inspired us in 1923 when we adopted the first ever Bill of Rights in this country. That same vision spurred us to put forward the African Claims in 1946. It is also the founding principle of the Freedom Charter we adopted as policy in 1955, which in its very first lines, places before South Africa an inclusive basis for citizenship.

In 1980s the African National Congress was still setting the pace, being the first major political formation in South Africa to commit itself firmly to a Bill of Rights, which we published in November 1990. These milestones give concrete expression to what South Africa can become. They speak of a constitutional, democratic, political order in which, regardless of colour, gender, religion, political opinion or sexual orientation, the law will provide for the equal protection of all citizens.

They project a democracy in which the government, whomever that government may be, will be bound by a higher set of rules, embodied in a constitution, and will not be able govern the country as it pleases.

Democracy is based on the majority principle. This is especially true in a country such as ours where the vast majority have been systematically denied their rights. At the same time, democracy also requires that the rights of political and other minorities be safeguarded.

In the political order we have established, there will regular, open and free elections, at all levels of government — central, provincial and municipal. There shall also be a social order which respects completely the culture, language and religious rights of all sections of our society and the fundamental rights of the individual.

The task at hand on will not be easy. But you have mandated us to change South Africa, from a country in which the majority lived with little hope, to one in which they can live and work with dignity, with a sense of self-esteem and confidence in the future. The cornerstone of building a better life of opportunity, freedom and prosperity is the Reconstruction and Development Programme.

This needs unity of purpose. It needs action. It requires us all to work together to bring an end to division, an end to suspicion, and build a nation united in our diversity.

The people of South Africa have spoken in these elections. They want change! And change is what they will get. Our plan is to create jobs, promote peace and reconciliation, and to guarantee freedom for all South Africans. We will tackle the widespread poverty so pervasive among the majority of our people. By encouraging investors and the democratic state to support job creating projects in which manufacturing will play a central role, we will try to change our country from a net exporter of raw materials to one that exports finished products through beneficiation.

The government will devise policies that encourage and reward productive enterprise among the disadvantaged communities—African, Coloured and Indian. By easing credit conditions we can assist them to make inroads into the productive and manufacturing spheres and breakout of the small-scale distribution to which they are presently confined.

To raise our country and its people from the morass of racism and apartheid will require determination and effort. As a government, the ANC will create a legal framework that will assist, rather than impede, the awesome task of reconstruction and development of our battered society.

While we are and shall remain fully committed to the spirit of a government of national unity, we are determined to initiate and bring about the change that our mandate from the people demands.

We place our vision of a new constitutional order for South Africa on the table not as conquerors, prescribing to the conquered. We speak as fellow citizens to heal the wounds of the past with the intent of constructing a new order based on justice for all.

This is the challenge that faces all South Africans today, and it is one to which I am certain we will all rise.

State Of The Nation

May 24, 1994

Madame Speaker and Deputy Speaker, President of the Senate and Deputy President, Deputy Presidents, Chief Justice, Distinguished members of the National Assembly and the Senate, Provincial Premiers, Commanders of the Security Forces, Members of the Diplomatic Corps, Esteemed guests, Comrades, Ladies and gentlemen.

The time will come when our nation will honour the memory of all the sons, the daughters, the mothers, the fathers, the youth and the children who, by their thoughts and deeds, gave us the right to assert with pride that we are South Africans, that we are Africans and that we are citizens of the world.

The certainties that come with age tell me that among these we shall find an Afrikaner woman who transcended a particular experience and became a South African, an African and a citizen of the world.

Her name is Ingrid Jonker.

She was both a poet and a South African. She was both an Afrikaner and an African. She was both an artist and a human being.

In the midst of despair, she celebrated hope. Confronted with death, she asserted the beauty of life.

In the dark days when all seemed hopeless in our country, when many refused to hear her resonant voice, she took her own life.

To her and others like her, we owe a debt to life itself. To her and others like her, we owe a commitment to the poor, the oppressed, the wretched and the despised.

In the aftermath of the massacre at the anti-pass demonstration in Sharpeville she wrote that:

"The child is not dead
the child lifts his fists against his mother
who shouts Africa!...

The child is not dead
Not at Langa nor at Nyanga
nor at Orlando nor at Sharpeville
nor at the police post at Philippi
where he lies with a bullet through his brain...

the child is present at all assemblies and law-giving
the child peers through the windows of houses
and into the hearts of mothers
this child who only wanted to play in the sun at Nyanga
is everywhere

the child grown to a man treks on through all Africa
the child grown to a giant journeys
over the whole world
without a pass!"

And in this glorious vision, she instructs that our endeavours must be about the liberation of the woman, the emancipation of the man and the liberty of the child.

It is these things that we must achieve to give meaning to our presence in this chamber and to give purpose to our occupancy of the seat of government.

And so we must, constrained by and yet regardless of the accumulated effect of our historical burdens, seize the time to define for ourselves what we want to make of our shared destiny.

The government I have the honour to lead and I dare say the masses who elected us to serve in this role, are inspired by the single vision of creating a people-centred society.

Accordingly, the purpose that will drive this government shall be the expansion of the frontiers of human fulfillment, the continuous extension of the frontiers of the freedom.

The acid test of the legitimacy of the programmes we elaborate, the government institutions we create, the legislation we adopt must be whether they serve these objectives.

Our single most important challenge is therefore to help establish a social order in which the freedom of the individual will truly mean the freedom of the individual.

We must construct that people-centred society of freedom in such a manner that it guarantees the political and the human rights of all our citizens.

As an affirmation of the government's commitment to an entrenched human rights culture, we shall immediately take steps to inform the Secretary General of the United Nations that we will subscribe to the Universal Declaration of Human Rights.

We shall take steps to ensure that we accede to the International Covenant on Civil and Political Rights, the International Covenant on Social and Economic Rights and other human rights instruments of the United Nations.

Our definition of the freedom of the individual must be instructed by the fundamental objective to restore the human dignity of each and every South African.

This requires that we speak not only of political freedoms.

My government's commitment to create a people-centred society of liberty binds us to the pursuit of the goals of freedom from want, freedom from hunger, freedom from deprivation, freedom from ignorance, freedom from suppression and freedom from fear.

These freedoms are fundamental to the guarantee of human dignity. They will therefore constitute part of the centrepiece of what this government will seek to achieve, the focal point on which our attention will be continuously focused.

The things we have said constitute the true meaning, the justification and the purpose of the Reconstruction and Development Programme, without which it would lose all legitimacy.

When we elaborated this Programme we were inspired by the hope that all South Africans of goodwill could join together to provide a better life for all. We were pleased that other political organisations announced similar aims.

Today, I am happy to announce that the Cabinet of the Government of National Unity has reached consensus not only on the broad objective of the creation of the people-centred society of which I have spoken, but also on many elements of a plan broadly based on that Programme for Reconstruction and Development.

Let me indicate some of the more important agreements. Annually, in the combined budgets of central government and the provinces, we will provide for an increasing amount of funding for the plan.

This will start with an appropriation of R2.5 billion in the 1994/95 budget that will be presented next month. This should rise to more than R10 billion by the fifth year of the life of this government.

Government will also use its own allocation of funds to the Reconstruction and Development Plan to exert maximum leverage in marshalling funds from within South Africa and abroad.

In this regard, I am pleased to report that we have been holding consultation with some of the principal business leaders of our country.

Consequently, we are assured that the business sector can and will make a significant contribution towards the structuring and management of such reconstruction and development funds, towards the effective identification and implementation of projects and by supporting the financing of the socio-economic development effort.

I am also pleased to report that many of our friends abroad have already made commitments to assist us to generate the reconstruction and development funds we need.

We thank them most sincerely for their positive attitude which arises not from objectives of charity but from the desire to express solidarity with the new society we seek to build.

We accept the duty of coordinating the management of the total resources that will be generated, without seeking to prescribe to other contributors or undermining the continued role of non-governmental organisations and community-based organisations.

The initial R2.5 billion will be found from savings and the redirection of spending, as included in the preliminary 1994/95 budget proposals presented to Cabinet.

I would like to thank the departments of state for their cooperation in carrying out this adjustment to their planning, at short notice.

As we allocate larger amount in future, we shall require further adjustments by departments, partly to correct the bias in the spending patterns which are a legacy of the past.

The longer period shall allow such changes to be properly planned. But they will still make great demands on the managerial capacity and spirit of cooperation of the Cabinet and the whole civil service.

We are confident that, motivated by the desire to serve the people, the public service will discharge its responsibilities with diligence, sensitivity and enthusiasm, among other things paying attention to the important goal of increasing efficiency and productivity.

My government is equally committed to ensure that we use this longer period properly fully to bring into the decision-making processes organs of civil society.

This will include the trade union movement and civic organisations, so that at no time should the government become isolated from the people. At the same time, steps will be taken to build the capacity of communities to manage their own affairs.

Precisely because we are committed to ensuring sustainable growth and development leading to a better life for all, we will continue existing programmes of fiscal rehabilitation.

We are therefore determined to make every effort to contain real general government consumption at present levels and to manage the budget deficit with a view to its continuous reduction.

Similarly, we are agreed that a permanently higher general level of taxation is to be avoided.

To achieve these important objectives will require consistent discipline on the part of both the central and the provincial governments.

Furthermore, this disciplined approach will ensure that we integrate the objectives of our Reconstruction and Development Plan within government expenditure and not treat them as incidental to the tasks of government, marginalised to the status of mere additions to the level of expenditure.

There are major areas of desperate need in our society.

As a signal of its seriousness to address these, the government will, within the next 100 days, implement various projects under the direct supervision of the President. Let me briefly mention these.

Children under the age of six and pregnant mothers will receive free medical care in every state hospital and clinic where such need exists. Similarly, a nutritional feeding scheme will be implemented in every primary school where such need is established. A concrete process of consultation between the major stakeholders in this area will be organised immediately.

A programme is already being implemented to electrify 350,000 homes during the current financial year.

A campaign will be launched at every level of government, a public works programme designed and all efforts made to involve the private sector, organised labour, the civics and other community organisations to rebuild our townships, restore services in rural and urban areas, while addressing the issue of job creation and training, especially for our unemployed youth.

Many details of the overall reconstruction and development plan remain to be discussed, agreed and put in place. But I believe that the broad outline I have given and the immediate initiatives I have mentioned, will allow you to share my joy at the progress already made by the Government of National Unity with regard to this important matter.

We shall carry out this plan within the context of a policy aimed at building a strong and growing economy which will benefit all our people.

I would like to deal with a few matters in this regard.

In support of sustainable economic growth and the macro-economic objective of Government, it will remain the primary objective of monetary policy to promote and maintain overall financial stability.

The Reserve Bank has the important function of protecting the value of our currency and striving for relative price stability at all times.

We are pleased that Dr Chris Stals will continue to serve as Governor of the Reserve Bank.

The battle to reduce the rate of inflation will continue. The realisation of many of our objectives for a fair and equal treatment of all our people will not be possible unless we succeed in avoiding high inflation in the economy.

We also face a major challenge in re-entering the global economy, while stable prices are vital to the restructuring of our industries and dealing with the critical issue of job-creation.

We are blessed with a heritage of a sophisticated financial sector. Our financial markets are well-placed to play an important part in the allocation of scarce funds to give effect to our economic development programme.

It is however also necessary that we think in new ways, to meet the challenges of reconstruction and development.

We therefore welcome recent developments that provide for the creation of community banks. We would also like to encourage the greater participation of established financial institutions in the important area of black economic empowerment and support for the development of small and medium business.

The latter two areas of economic activity will receive the greatest attention of the Government because of their importance in deracialising and democratising the economy and creating the jobs which our people need.

We pay attention to the important matter of consumer protection to shield the ordinary people of our country from unscrupulous business practices.

We must also clear that we must pay increased attention to tourism. The jobs and foreign currency which tourism generates will strongly influence our economy.

The active and imaginative intervention of all stake stakeholders in this area of our national life must take advantage of the excellent atmosphere created by our peaceful transition to democracy to make tourism a major positive force in the future.

We look forward to the private sector as a whole playing a central role in achieving the significantly high and sustainable rates of economic growth.

We are convinced that the growth prospects of this sector will be enhanced by the measures of fiscal discipline contained in our approach to the Reconstruction and Development Programme and by the continued steady course of monetary policy.

As growth proceeds, more domestic savings will progressively become available to finance increased investment at reasonable rates of interest.

The Government is also acutely conscious of the fact that we should work firstly to return the capital account of the balance of payments to equilibrium and, in due course, to ensure a net inflow of resources, consistent with the experience of other countries that enjoy more rapid growth rates.

The present situation of a dual currency and the existence of an exchange control apparatus is a direct result of the conflict in which our country was embroiled in the past.

As the situation returns to normal, these arrangements will be subjected to critical scrutiny. It should be possible to match the steady growth of confidence at home and abroad with other confidence enhancing modifications to everybody's benefit.

The Government will also address all other matters that relate the creation of an attractive investment climate for both domestic and foreign investors, conscious of the fact that we have to compete with the rest of the world in terms of attracting, in particular, foreign direct investment.

I am pleased that we have already started to address the important question of our trade policy, guided by our GATT commitments and the determination systematically to open the economy to global competition in a carefully managed process.

Soon we will also begin trade negotiations with, among others, the European Union, the United States, our partners in the Southern African Customs Unions and our neighbours in the Southern African Development Community to provide a stable and mutually beneficial framework for our international economic relations.

We will also be looking very closely at the question of enhancing South-South cooperation in general as part of the effort to expand our economic links with the rest of the world.

Consistent with our objective of creating a people-centred society and effectively to address the critical questions of growth, reconstruction and development, we will, together with organised labour and the private sector, pay special attention to the issue of human resource development.

Both the public and the private sectors will be encouraged to regard labour as a resource and not a cost. Education and training must therefore be looked at very closely to ensure that we empower the workers, raise productivity levels and meet the skills needs of a modern economy.

Important work will have to be done in and significant resources devoted to the areas of science and technology, including research and development.

Government is also convinced that organised labour is an important partner whose cooperation is crucial for the reconstruction and development of our country.

That partnership requires, among other things, that our labour law be reformed so that it is in line with international standards, apartheid vestiges are removed and a more harmonious labour relations dispensation is created, on the basis of tripartite cooperation between government, labour and capital.

The Government is determined forcefully to confront the scourge of unemployment, not by way of handouts but by the creation of work opportunities.

The Government will also deal sensitively with the issue of population movements into the country, to protect our workers, to guard against the exploitation of vulnerable workers and to ensure friendly relations with all countries and peoples.

The Government is also taking urgent measures to deal firmly with drug trafficking some of which is carried out by foreign nationals who are resident in the country.

We must end racism in the workplace as part of our common offensive against racism in general. No more should words like Kaffirs, Hottentots, Coolies, Boy, Girl and Baas be part of our vocabulary.

I also trust that the matter of paying the workers for the public holidays proclaimed in order to ensure their participation in the elections and the inauguration ceremonies will now be resolved as a result of recent consultations.

This would be a welcome demonstration by the private sector of its involvement in the beautiful future we are all trying to build.

We have devoted time to a discussion of economic questions because they are fundamental to the realisation of the fundamental objectives of the reconstruction and development programme

Below I mention some of the work in which the relevant governments are already involved to translate these objectives into reality.

The Government will take steps to ensure the provision of clean water on the basis of the principle of water security for all and the introduction of proper sanitation sensitive to the protection of the environment.

We are determined to address the dire housing shortage in a vigorous manner, acting together with the private sector and the communities in need of shelter.

Health also remains a fundamental building block of the humane society we are determined to create through the implementation of the Reconstruction and Development Programme.

We must address the needs of the aged and disabled, uplift disadvantaged sectors such as the women and the youth, and improve the lives of our people in the rural communities and the informal settlements.

We must invest substantial amounts in education and training and meet our commitment to introduce free and compulsory education for a period of at least 9 years. Everywhere we must reinculcate the culture of learning and of teaching and make it possible for this culture to thrive.

We must combat such social pathologies as widespread poverty, the break down of family life, crime, alcohol and drug abuse, the abuse of children, women and the elderly, and the painful reality of street children. We are giving urgent attention to the long waiting lists for the payment of social grants which have developed in some areas, owing to lack of funds.

I am especially pleased that we have a ministry dedicated to the issue of the environment. Its work must impact on many aspects of national activity and address the question of the well-being of society as a whole and the preservation of a healthy environmental future even for generation not yet born.

As we began this address, we borrowed the words of Ingrid Jonker to focus on the plight of the children our country.

I would now like to say that the Government will, as a matter of urgency, attend to the tragic and complex question of children and juveniles in detention and prison.

The basic principle from which we will proceed from now onwards is that we must rescue the children of the nation and ensure that the system of criminal justice must be the very last resort in the case of juvenile offenders.

I have therefore issued instruction to the Departments concerned, as a matter of urgency, to work out the necessary guidelines which will enable us to empty our prisons of children and to place them in suitable alternative care. This is in addition to an amnesty for various categories of serving prisoners as will be effected in terms of what I said in my Inauguration Address two weeks ago.

In this context, I also need to make the point that the Government will also not delay unduly with regard to attending to the vexed and unresolved issue of an amnesty for criminal activities carried out in furtherance of political objectives.

We will attend to this matter in a balanced and dignified way. The nation must come to terms with its past in a spirit of openness and forgiveness and proceed to build the future on the basis of repairing and healing.

The burden of the past lies heavily on all of us, including those responsible for inflicting injury and those who suffered.

Following the letter and the spirit of the Constitution, we will prepare the legislation which will seek to free the wrongdoers from fear of retribution and blackmail, while acknowledging the injury of those who have been harmed so that the individual wrongs, injuries, fears and hopes affecting individuals are identified and attended to.

In the meantime, summoning the full authority of the position we represent, we call on all concerned not to take any steps that might, in any way, impede or compromise the processes of reconciliation which the impending legislation will address.

The problem of politically motivated violence is still with us. We depend on our country's security forces to deal with this problem, using all resources at their disposal. In this, and in their efforts to deal especially criminal violence, they have our personal support and confidence.

We have also directed that all relevant ministries should engage the structures set up in terms of the National Peace Accord so that these can be invigorated to pursue their noble mission in the context of the changed circumstances in our country.

The Government will otherwise not spare any effort in ensuring that our security forces enjoy the standing they deserve of being accepted by all our people the defenders of our sovereignty, our democratic system, the guarantors of a just peace within the country and the safety and security of all citizens and their property.

Let met also take this opportunity to reiterate our assurance to the rest of the public service that the Government is firmly committed to the protection of the rights of all members of this service.

We are also determined to work with the organisations of the service to ensure that we have the democratic, non-racial, non-sexist, honest and accountable corps of public servants which members of the Public Service themselves desire.

In this context, we must also make the observation that the Government will not waver from the principle of achieving parity in remuneration and conditions of service among all workers in the public sector.

The youth of our country are the valued possession of the nation. Without them there can be no future. Their needs are immense and urgent. They are at the centre of our reconstruction and development plan.

To address them, acting with the youth themselves, the Government will engage the representative organisations of the youth and other formations, among other things to look at the siting of a broad-based National Commission on Youth Development among the structures of Government.

Building on this base, the Government and the Commission would then work together to ensure that the nurturing of our youth stands at the centre of our reconstruction and development, without being consigned to a meaningless ghetto of public life.

Similar considerations must attach to the equally important question of the emancipation of the women of our country.

It is vitally important that all structures of Government, including the President himself, should understand this fully, that freedom cannot be achieved unless the women have been emancipated from all forms of oppression.

All of us must take this on board, that the objectives of the Reconstruction and Development Programme will not have been realised unless we see in visible and practical terms that the condition of the women of our country has radically changed for the better and that they have been empowered to intervene in all aspects of life as equals with any other member of society.

In addition to the establishment of the statutory Gender Commission provided for in the Constitution, the Government will, together with the representatives of the women themselves, look at the establishment of organs of Government to ensure that all levels of the public sector, from top to bottom, integrate the central issue of the emancipation of women in their programmes and daily activities.

Tomorrow, on Africa Day, the dream of Ingrid Jonker will come to fruition. The child grown to a man will trek through all Africa. The child grown to a journey will journey over the whole world — without a pass!

Tomorrow, on Africa Day, our new flag will be hoisted in an historic ceremony at the OAU Headquarters in Addis Ababa, with the OAU having already agreed to accept us as its latest member.

Tomorrow, on Africa Day, the UN Security Council will meet to lift the last remaining sanctions against South Africa and to position the world organisation to relate to our country as an honoured, responsible and peace-loving citizen.

As such, the Government is involved in discussion to determine what our contribution could be to the search for peace in Angola and Rwanda, to the reinforcement of the peace process in Mozambique, to the establishment of a new world order of mutually beneficial cooperation, justice, prosperity and peace for ourselves and for the nations of the world.

Yesterday the Cabinet also decided to apply for our country to join the Commonwealth. This important community of nations is waiting to receive us with open arms.

We have learnt the lesson that our blemishes speak of what all humanity should not do. We understand this fully that our glories point to the heights of what human genius can achieve.

In our dreams we have a vision of all our country at play in our sports fields and enjoying deserved and enriching recreation in our theatres, galleries, beaches, mountains, plains and game parks, in conditions of peace, security and comfort.

Our road to that glorious future lies through collective hard work to accomplish the objective of creating a people-centred society through the implementation of the vision contained in our reconstruction and development plan.

Let us all get down to work!

Statement At The OAU

June 13, 1994

Mr Chairman, Distinguished Heads of State and Government, Heads of Delegations, Your Excellencies, Ministers, Ambassadors and High Commissioner, Comrades, Ladies and Gentlemen.

In the distant days of antiquity, a Roman sentenced this African city to death: "Carthage must be destroyed (*Carthago delenda est*)".

And Carthage was destroyed. Today we wander among its ruins, only our imagination and historical records enable us to experience its magnificence. Only our African being makes it possible for us to hear the piteous cries of the victims of the vengeance of the Roman Empire.

And yet we can say this, that all human civilisation rests on foundations such as the ruins of the African city of Carthage. These architectural remains, like the pyramids of Egypt, the sculptures of the ancients kingdoms of Ghana and Mali and Benin, like the temples of Ethiopia, the Zimbabwe ruins and the rock paintings of the Kgalagadi and Namib deserts, all speak of

Africa's contribution to the formation of the condition of civilisation.

But in the end, Carthage was destroyed. During the long interregnum, the children of Africa were carted away as slaves. Our lands became the property of other nations, our resources a source of enrichment for other peoples, and our kings and queens mere servants of foreign powers.

In the end, we were held out as the outstanding example of the beneficiaries of charity, because we became the permanent victims of famine, of destructive conflicts, and of the pestilence of the natural world. On our knees because history, society and nature had defeated us, we could be nothing but beggars. What the Romans had sought with the destruction of Carthage, had been achieved.

But the ancient pride of the peoples of our continent asserted itself and gave us hope in the form of giants such as Queen Regent Labotsibeni of Swaziland, Mohammed V of Morocco, Abdul Gamal Nasser of Egypt, Kwame Nkrumah of Ghana, Murtala Mohammed of Nigeria, Patrice Lumumba of Zaire, Amilcar Cabral of Guinea Bissau, Aghostino Neto of Angola, Eduardo Mondlane and Samora Machel of Mozambique, Seretse Khama of Botswana, WEB Du Bois and Martin Luther King of America, Marcus Garvey of Jamaica, Albert Luthuli and Oliver Tambo of South Africa.

By their deeds, by the struggles they led, these and many other patriots said to us that neither Carthage nor Africa had been destroyed. They conveyed the message that the long interregnum of humiliation was over. It is in their honour that we stand here today. It is a tribute to their heroism that, today, we are able to address this august gathering.

The titanic effort that has brought liberation to South Africa, and ensured the total liberation of Africa, constitutes an act of redemption for the black people of the world. It is a gift of emancipation also to those who, because they were white, imposed on themselves the heavy burden of assuming the mantle of rulers of all humanity. It says to all who will listen and understand that, by ending the apartheid barbarity that was the offspring of European colonisation, Africa has, once more, contributed to the advance of human civilization, and further expanded the frontiers of liberty everywhere.

We are here today not to thank you, dear brothers and sisters, because such thanks would be misplaced among fellow-combatants — we are here to salute and congratulate you for a most magnificent and historical victory over an inhuman system whose very name was tyranny, injustice and bigotry.

When the history of our struggle is written, it will tell a glorious tale of African solidarity, of African's adherence to principles. It will tell a moving story of the sacrifices that the peoples of our continent made, to ensure that that intolerable insult to human dignity, the apartheid crime against humanity, became a thing of the past. It will speak of the contributions of freedom — whose value is as measureless as the gold beneath the soil of our country — the contribution which all of Africa made, from the shores of the Mediterranean Sea in the north, to the confluence of the Indian and Atlantic Oceans in the north.

Africa shed her blood and surrendered the lives of her children so that all her children could be free. She gave of her limited wealth and resources so that all of Africa should be liberated. She opened heart of hospitality and her head so full of wise counsel, so that we should emerge victorious. A million times, she put her hand to the plough that has now dug up the encrusted burden of oppression accumulated for centuries.

The total liberation of Africa from foreign and white minority rule has now been achieved. Our colleagues who have served with distinction on the OAU liberation committee have already carried out the historical task of winding up this institution, which we shall always remember as a frontline fighter for the emancipation of the people of our continent.

Finally, at this summit meeting in Tunis, we shall remove from our agenda the consideration of the question of Apartheid South Africa.

Where South Africa appears on the agenda again, let it be because we want to discuss what its contribution shall be to the making of the new African renaissance. Let it be because we want to discuss what materials it will supply for the rebuilding of the African city of Carthage.

One epoch with its historic tasks has come to an end. Surely, another must commence with its own challenges. Africa cries out for a new birth, Carthage awaits the restoration of its glory.

If freedom was the crown which the fighters of liberation sought to place on the head of mother Africa, let the upliftment, the happiness, prosperity and comfort of her children be the jewel of the crown.

There can be no dispute among us that we must bend every effort to rebuild the African economies. You, your excellencies, have discussed this matter many times and elaborated the ideas whose implementation would lead us to success.

The fundamentals of what needs to be done are known to all of us. Not least among these are the need to address the reality that Africa continues to be a net exporter of capital and suffers from deteriorating terms of trade. Our capacity to be self-reliant, to find the internal resources to generate sustained development, remains very limited.

Quite correctly, we have also spent time discussing the equally complex questions that bear on the nature and quality of governance. These, too, are central to our capacity to produce the better life which our people demand and deserve. In this regard, we surely must face the matter squarely that where there is something wrong in the manner in which we govern ourselves, it must be said that the fault is not in our stars, but in ourselves that we are ill-governed.

Tribute is due to the great thinkers of our continent who have been and are trying to move all of us to understand the intimate inter-connection between the great issues of our day of peace, stability, democracy, human rights, co-operation and development.

Even as we speak, Rwanda stands out as a stern and severe rebuke to all of us for having failed to address these interrelated matters. As a result of that, a terrible slaughter of the innocent is taking place in front of our very eyes.

Thus do we give reason to the peoples of the world to say of Africa that she will never know stability and peace, that she will never experience development and growth, that her children will forever be condemned to poverty and dehumanisation and that we shall for ever be knocking on somebody's door pleading for a slice of bread.

We know it is a matter of fact that we have it in ourselves as Africans to change all this. We must, in action, assert our will to do so. We must, in action, say that there is no obstacle big enough to stop us from bringing about a new African renaissance.

We are happy, Mr Chairman, to commit South Africa to the achievement of these goals. We have entered this eminent African organisation and rejoined the African community of nations inspired by the desire to join hands with all the countries of our continent as equal partners.

It will never happen again that our country should seek to dominate another through force of arms, economic might or subversion. We are determined to remain true to the vision which you held out for South Africa as you joined the offensive to destroy the system of apartheid.

The vision you shared with us was one of a non-racial society, whose very being would assert the ancient African values of respect for every person and commitment to the elevation of human dignity, regardless of colour or race.

What we all aimed for was a South Africa which would succeed in banishing the ethnic and national conflicts which continue to plague our continent. What we, together, hoped to see, was a new South Africa freed of conflict among its people and the violence that has taken such a heavy toll, freed of the threat of the civil strife that has turned millions of people into refugees both inside and outside our countries.

We all prayed and sacrificed to bring about a South Africa that we could hold out as a true example of the democracy, equality and justice for all, which the apartheid system was constructed and intended to deny.

The vision you shared with us was one in which we would use the resources of our country to create a society in which all our people would be emancipated from the scourges of poverty, disease, ignorance and backwardness.

The objective we pursued was the creation of a South Africa that would be a good neighbour and an equal partner with all the countries of our continent, one which would use its abilities and potentialities to help advance the common struggle to secure Africa's rightful place within the world economic and political system.

Thus must we build on the common victory of the total emancipation of Africa to obtain new successes for our continent as a whole.

Mr Chairman:

We are ready to contribute what we can to help end the genocide that is taking place in Rwanda and bring peace to that troubled sister country.

We also join the distinguished Heads of State and Government and Leaders of Delegations in urging a speedy implementation of the OAU and UN decisions aimed at resolving the question of Western Sahara.

We extend our best wishes to the leaders and people of Angola in the fervent hope that the process of negotiations in which they are engaged will, as a matter of urgency, bring about the permanent and just peace which the people of that country so richly deserve.

Equally, we would like to express our deep-felt wish that the necessary measures will be taken by all concerned to guarantee the success of the peace processes in Mozambique and Liberia, to end the war in the Sudan, and protect democracy and stability in Lesotho.

We also appeal to the world community to respond in a sensitive and generous manner to the famine that threatens the peoples of East Africa.

Mr Chairman, our delegation is also happy to announce that we have had the honour to pay the subscription that the OAU has levied for South Africa. In addition, and as a token of the commitment of the people of our country to support Africa's peace efforts, we are glad to inform the Assembly that we have also made an additional contribution of R1 million to the OAU fund for peace.

We congratulate you, Mr Chairman, on your election as the current chairman of the OAU and thank you, your government and people for the extraordinary welcome you have extended to us. We are indeed glad to be here because Tunisia was among the first countries on our continent to respond to our appeal for help, when we were obliged to take up arms to fight for our liberation.

We thank our brother, President Hosni Mubarak, for the outstanding work he did during his chairpersonship, including the direction of the efforts of the OAU as it helped us to deal with political violence in our country and ensure the holding of free and fair elections.

We salute too, our Secretary-General, HE Salim Ahmed Salim, the OAU Secretariat, the OAU Head of Mission to South Africa, Ambassador Joe Legwaila, the Heads of State and Government and the people of our continent who helped us successfully to walk our last mile of the difficult road to freedom.

To you all, we would like to say that your sacrifices and your efforts have not been in vain. Freedom for Africa is your reward. Your actions entitled you to be saluted as the heroes and heroines of our time. On your shoulders rests the responsibility to restore to our continent its dignity.

We are certain that you will prevail over the currents that originate from the past, and ensure that the interregnum of humiliation symbolised by, among others, the destruction of Charthage, is indeed consigned to the past, never to return.

God bless Africa.

Thank you.

Address On The Anniversary Of The Soweto Uprising

June 16, 1994

Master of Ceremonies, Honourable Ministers of the Government of National Unity, Honourable Provincial Premiers and cabinet members, Leaders of political parties, Leaders of the various youth organizations, Comrades and friends

When the tragic events of 16 June 1976 erupted in Soweto, the question posed itself to the whole of South Africa: So Where to Now? In the sacrifices that were borne by Hector Peterson and many other young people, there seemed to lie an answer. That the destiny of the youth was the grave and the hangman's noose, detention and long terms of imprisonment, exile and banishment.

That is what those who arrogated to themselves the status of slave-master sought to achieve. In the false comfort of their ill-gotten power, they convinced themselves that the answer to South Africa's problems was to murder, to maim and to persecute. But they had typically closed their eyes to the historical truth that it is a God-given right that the slave should revolt. To the question, So Where to Now, the answer of the youth and people of South Africa was: to battle, to struggle, to more bravery. Today, we mark the 18th anniversary of June 16th as a free people, proud and full of joy for taking the resistance of that generation and others before and after it to its final conclusion. Yet we mark this day also with a feeling of sadness: that the thousands who deserve to be here with us today are no more. We salute them all.

We commemorate this day, not with the song of defiance on our lips. This is no longer a day of protest by an excluded majority.

We have elected a government of our choice, at the head of which is the African National Congress.

The brave young people of that generation are today eminent premiers, ministers and members of national and provincial parliaments. They are taking their rightful place in the ranks of the new South African National Defence Force and other institutions of state and civil society.

Our presence together here—as representatives of the Government of National Unity, various political parties, youth organisations and structures of workers and communities—symbolises the fact that this is truly a national day.

The Government is reviewing all South Africa's holidays, to ensure that our calendar is reflective of the total experience of all the people. And to us it is patently clear what the mandate is from this gathering and many others throughout the country. With regard to today, in particular, we urge that employers honour agreements with workers regarding June 16th as a paid holiday. But we would be misrepresenting the sentiments of the Class of '76 if our only concern was that this day should be declared a national holiday.

Rather, we should first and foremost, approach it from the point of view that the heroes of those struggles had a noble mission. They were inspired by a thirst for knowledge:

knowledge which knows no colour;

knowledge acquired through persuasion and hard work;

knowledge that taps talents and releases creative energies; and

knowledge that puts South African youth on par with the best in the world.

As we enter the new and glorious epoch that June 16th helped to usher in, we will do well to emulate that heroism and turn it into an asset for the tasks that lie ahead.

We have achieved our freedom. But formal liberation will be an empty shell if we do not immediately start addressing the social conditions bred by apartheid. The Reconstruction and Development Programme must be implemented without delay.

It is therefore fitting that youth organisations of various persuasions have adopted the theme: Youth United for Reconciliation, Education and Development—as an embodiment of the spirit of this commemoration. We also acknowledge the presence in our midst of eminent representatives of the United Nations International Children's Education Fund; and express our confidence that your presence in our country will, in more ways than one, assist our programmes to improve the conditions of our youth.

The Government is convinced that among the first challenges that we need to address in this regard is to inculcate the culture of learning and teaching in all schools.

No matter what the origins of the profound education crisis might be, the fact is that this has become our collective heritage.

We are no longer petitioners, exerting pressure from the sidelines.

We have to roll up our sleeves and together tackle the problems.

I am personally encouraged by reports of a return to normality in the schools, since the elections. This does show the commitment on the part of teachers and students to expend their energies in ensuring that we truly become masters of our own destiny.

The problems wrought by apartheid education have lately been compounded by such terrible tendencies as the proliferation of criminal gangs, weapons and drugs in some of our schools. This cannot be allowed to continue. All-round discipline, within an education strategy involving all players, is fundamental to the solution of these problems.

In order to address the root causes of the education crisis, we intend to table a Bill in parliament soon, to eradicate discrimination and take the first major steps towards ten years of free quality education.

For these changes to be effective, there has to be close co-operation between government and organisations of teachers, students, parents, workers and the business community. The task to make South Africa a learning and learned nation belongs to all of us.

The culture of teaching and learning means also that there should be a culture of rights in the schools. Teachers deserve to be treated with respect by students, society and government. In turn, they will enjoy such respect if they act responsibly, appreciating the central position that their fraternity occupies in society.

With regard to this year in particular, we fully support the initiatives to make up for the time lost during recent national events. We hope that the intensive learning effort will constitute the beginning of a nation-wide and continuing campaign.

The opening of doors to the world offers more than just new opportunities for the youth. It is also a great challenge for us to improve our standards to match those of other nations.

I wish to use this opportunity to send out an invitation to the youth of our country to be a full part of the exciting transformation that we are engaged in. The government is involved in discussions with different youth organisations on how they can best make their contribution to the nation-building and development effort.

During the address at the opening of the last session of parliament, we announced the decision to establish a National Youth Commission. We have now gone a step further and established a Cabinet Committee on Youth under the supervision of Minister of Sport and Recreation. We further wish to welcome the progress being made by the youth formations towards the setting up of a youth parliament in the form of the National Youth Council.

In these endeavours, political youth organisations in particular need to address the problem of their functioning simply as duplicates of their mother bodies. Needless to say, what is needed are creative programmes which promote the interests of all youth and involve African, Coloured, Indian and white youth.

In so far as government is concerned, the aim is not to attend to the youth as if you were some separate and special species from outer space. Our central approach is to ensure that young people are fully integrated into the social, economic and political life of society.

Our policies must turn into reality the principle that every child deserves to have a decent home and be brought up in the loving care of a family. The terrible legacy of street children has to be attended to with urgency. A collective effort has to be launched by the government, civil society and the private sector to ensure that every child is looked after, has sufficient nutrition and health care. The government has already started taking steps in this regard.

We have, further, taken steps to ensure that within the shortest possible time, we empty our jails of children. The process of finding alternative centres for them is under way.

Personally, I regard this as an urgent priority. In a humble attempt to contribute to this effort, I am consulting with relevant individuals and bodies, for me to set up a Presidential

Trust Fund representative of people beyond the ANC and the mass democratic movement, to specifically deal with the problems of street children and detainees. I intend to make a contribution of R150,000 a year to this fund — irrespective of the decision that parliament will make about the salaries of elected representatives. Further details will be announced in due course.

The Fund I have referred to will assist in alleviating these problems. But I do recognise, as all of you do, that a lasting solution lies in comprehensive socio-economic upliftment programmes. At the same time, the youth, especially from disadvantaged communities, need to realise that we cannot rely only on governmental programmes and charity. We also have to take initiatives in our communities to pool our meagre resources for projects such as bursaries and skills upgrading.

One of the most important problems facing the youth and society is the AIDS epidemic and we can no longer afford to hide behind tradition and embarrassment, pretending that this problem does not exist. To do so is to consign our nation to certain disaster. We need to join hands now to ensure that the campaigns launched make the maximum impact.

It serves no purpose to continue blaming the past for these problems, including drug trafficking, gangsterism and violence. We must all take responsibility by tackling the root causes at the same time as we ensure effective law-enforcement.

The security forces, working hand-in-hand with communities, have an enormous role to play in this regard.

The responsibility of maintaining public safety and security is not one of the police alone. The people more especially the youth should take an active part in the police-community forums that are being set up across the country. And, together, we must transform the institutions of security to become servants of the people. For this reason, we should all condemn in the strongest terms the shooting and killing of policemen and women.

In addition, our communities cannot allow a situation in which young men and women continue to harass communities and butcher one another in the name of community self-defence.

We are convinced that there are many cadres of integrity in self-defence units who have played a crucial role in times of need. But the true measure of their integrity has been displayed in their co-operation with community structures to implement a programme that will see to their return to school, integration within the security forces or participation in skills-upgrading. Those who defy these programmes cannot justifiably claim to act on behalf of the community or expect community protection for their evil deeds.

I call on all youth to join us in the effort to build peace and reconciliation in our land.

The Government of National Unity is on course and all the participating organisations are co-operating well. As demonstrated at the OAU Summit from which we have just returned, we are, as a nation, making a tremendous impact on the continent and the entire world.

The manner in which the youth co-ordinating structures have organised this event is a clear statement to the nation and the world, that the youth is committed to the healing of the wounds of the past.

With you, we say to all South Africa's youth, black and white, including those in the army and police: June 16th is your day. You might have been on the other side of the dividing line of apartheid. But now is the time to join the majority in building a new and glorious future for our country and all its people.

There is nothing to fear from democracy. The African National Congress seeks no retribution. Our message of reconciliation is inspired by a genuine love for our country. When we call for the truth we do so in order to ensure that all of us come to terms with the past. So that we can bury those evil experiences secure in the knowledge that future generations will recoil from any temptation to repeat them.

Let us all rise to the challenge of the freedom that we have won. That challenge is to create a better life for all South Africans: to create jobs, to provide free quality education and open up opportunities for skills training, to build houses, to provide health facilities and other basic services.

Let us together answer the question, So Where to Now, with a new youthful determination to learn, to build and to live life to the full. The country thirsts for your talents and energy.

Together, let us get South Africa working!

Thank you.

CPSIA information can be obtained at www.ICGtesting.com
Printed in the USA
LVOW030858030112

262154LV00006B/128/P